THE SHETLAND
SHEEPDOG

Sheila Webster Boneham, Ph.D.

The Shetland Sheepdog

Project Team
Editor: Mary E. Grangeia
Copy Editor: Joann Woy
Indexer: Elizabeth Walker
Design: Patti Escabi
Series Design: Stephanie Krautheim and Mada Design
Series Originator: Dominique De Vito

T.F.H. Publications
President/CEO: Glen S. Axelrod
Executive Vice President: Mark E. Johnson
Publisher: Christopher T. Reggio
Production Manager: Kathy Bontz

T.F.H. Publications, Inc.
One TFH Plaza
Third and Union Avenues
Neptune City, NJ 07753

ISBN 978-0-7938-3690-1

Printed and bound in China
10 11 12 13 14   3 5 7 9 8 6 4 2

Library of Congress Cataloging-in-Publication Data
Boneham, Sheila Webster, 1952-.
   The Shetland sheepdog / Sheila Webster Boneham.
      p. cm.
   Includes index.
   ISBN 978-0-7938-3690-1 (alk. paper)
   1. Shetland sheepdog. I. Title.
   SF429.S62B66 2010
   636.737—dc22
                                2009033069

This book has been published with the intent to provide accurate and authoritative information in regard to the subject matter within. While every reasonable precaution has been taken in preparation of this book, the author and publisher expressly disclaim responsibility for any errors, omissions, or adverse effects arising from the use or application of the information contained herein. The techniques and suggestions are used at the reader's discretion and are not to be considered a substitute for veterinary care. If you suspect a medical problem consult your veterinarian.

Note: In the interest of concise writing, "he" is used when referring to puppies and dogs unless the text is specifically referring to females or males. "She" is used when referring to people. However, the information contained herein is equally applicable to both sexes.

The Leader In Responsible Animal Care For Over 50 Years.®
www.tfh.com

TABLE OF CONTENTS

Chapter 1

HISTORY OF THE SHETLAND SHEEPDOG 5

The Dog of the Isles • Breed History in Great Britain • Breed History in the United States • Dogs and People Who Influenced the Breed

Chapter 2

CHARACTERISTICS OF THE SHETLAND SHEEPDOG 13

Standards of Perfection • Size and Substance • Form Follows Function • Clothed in Elegance • Temperament and Behavior • The Right Dog in the Right Place • Shelties and Children • Shelties and Other Pets

Chapter 3

PREPARING FOR YOUR SHETLAND SHEEPDOG 31

Puppy or Adult? • Sheltie Boy or Sheltie Girl? • Pet, Performance, or Show Dog? • Finding Your Shetland Sheepdog • New Dog Paperwork • Pick of the Litter • The Best Time to Bring Your Puppy Home • Preparing Your Home and Yard • Shopping for Your Sheltie • Traveling—or Not—With Your Sheltie • The Importance of Planning Ahead

Chapter 4

FEEDING YOUR SHETLAND SHEEPDOG 55

Basic Canine Nutrition • Commercial Dog Foods • Noncommercial Diets • When to Feed Your Sheltie • Slim and Trim, or Roly Poly? • Less is More

Chapter 5

GROOMING YOUR SHETLAND SHEEPDOG 75

Benefits of Good Grooming • Grooming Supplies • Coat Care • Dental Care • Ear Care • Eye Care • Foot and Nail Care • How to Find a Professional Groomer

Chapter 6

TRAINING AND BEHAVIOR OF YOUR SHETLAND SHEEPDOG 93

Why Train Your Sheltie? • Getting Off on the Right Paw • Socialization • Crate Training • Housetraining • Leash Training • Going to Doggy School • Four Commands Your Sheltie Should Know • Getting a Grip on Problem Behaviors

Chapter 7

ADVANCED TRAINING AND ACTIVITIES FOR YOUR SHETLAND SHEEPDOG 131

Fun and Fitness: Noncompetitive Activities • Good Dogs, Good Works • Beauty Is as Beauty Does: Performance Sports for Shetland Sheepdogs

Chapter 8

HEALTH OF YOUR SHETLAND SHEEPDOG 153

Partnering With Your Veterinarian • Routine Veterinary Care • Infectious Diseases and Vaccinations • Controlling Parasites • Hormones, Health, and Behavior • Health Issues in Shetland Sheepdogs • Alternative Therapies • Emergency Care and First Aid • Your Senior Sheltie • Saying Goodbye

RESOURCES 198

INDEX 202

1

HISTORY

of the Shetland Sheepdog

To understand some of the physical and behavioral traits of your Sheltie companion, it's important to learn something of his historical roots. The Shetland Sheepdog (Sheltie) of today is descended from tough little working dogs developed in the Shetland Islands. Like most modern breeds, the Sheltie's early ancestors were not just companions for their human owners, but vital working partners. Because the traits that enabled them to do their assigned jobs in the harsh environment of the Shetland Islands are still found in their present-day descendents, knowing something about their ancestral background will help you to better interact with your Sheltie so that he can become a well-adjusted and happy member of your family.

THE DOG OF THE ISLES

The Shetland Islands lie just south of the Arctic Circle, some 50 miles (81 km) north of Scotland. Winters are long and harsh, and summers are short. The rocky, windblown terrain supports only sparse vegetation. Both food and space are limited, and many of the animals developed and raised in the Shetlands are smaller than their mainland counterparts— Shetland cattle and sheep and, better known to most people, Shetland ponies. And, of course, the Shetland Sheepdog.

The traditional Shetland crofters (small tenant farmers) long favored these small, smart collie-type working dogs for many jobs, including keeping livestock out of their precious home gardens and tending flocks left to forage on uninhabited islands. Their physical traits reflected the landscape in which they developed. Double-coated for warmth and weather-proofing, the Sheltie's long, flowing outer coat repelled the cold rain and blocked the wind, and his soft undercoat insulated the skin. His small size, sturdiness, and tremendous agility were suited for working sheep in rocky territory, as well as for easy keeping. Eventually, the Sheltie was brought from his home islands to the mainland and began to gain some notoriety as a herding dog and companion.

Early Development of the Breed

The Shetland Islanders were traditionally tenant farmers and fishermen who harvested small crops from tiny gardens on their small farms, called toons, and let their livestock roam free in search of forage. Unfortunately, crops meant for human consumption were often the easiest forage. During the mid 1800s, islanders began keeping small agile dogs, called Toonies, who were good at driving livestock away from these precious sources of food. Records suggest that these dogs were "pretty, intelligent, and hardy," and very small, at 10 to 11 inches (25 to 28 cm) tall and weighing 6 to 10 lbs (2.7 to 4.5 kg). Although the ancestry of the Toonie is lost in the mists of history, it likely included an older, larger indigenous herding dog, as well as imported working Collies from the mainland and various other dogs brought in from other parts of Europe.

By the end of the nineteenth century, many of these little island dogs were being taken away by visitors, particularly tourists and whalers, and Shetland farmers were beginning to favor larger herding dogs as the structure of their island economy changed. Concerned that the traditional Toonie would disappear, a number of dog fanciers in Scotland and England set out to preserve the traditional island dogs. As is often the case, though, they disagreed about exactly what qualities they should preserve or improve.

Some fanciers wanted to preserve the tiny version of the Toonie by selecting and crossing the best dogs they could find on the islands. Others crossed Toonies with small Rough Collies (which were similar to today's "farm Collie") with an eye to strengthening the finest traits and expanding the gene pool at the same

What Is a Collie Dog?

The term "collie" comes from a British word meaning "useful." Hence a "collie dog" was originally a dog who made himself useful, especially on farms. The term gradually came to denote specific types and then breeds of dog, some of which still have "collie" in their names, and some of which do not, such as the Shetland Sheepdog. Those dogs who retain the word "collie" in their breed names vary from place to place, however. For example, in the United States, "Collie" refers primarily to the breed known in Britain as the "Rough Collie." Similarly, the breed known as the "Collie" in Britain is called a "Border Collie" in the United States. Regardless, collie dogs of all types continue to maintain their longstanding reputation as beautiful, intelligent, and devoted working dogs and companions.

The Shetland Sheepdog of today is descended from tough little working dogs developed in the Shetland Islands.

time. Although crossbreeding of dogs is generally frowned upon today, the Kennel Club did allow the practice of "declared crosses" at the time. The resulting dog, who was a bit bigger than the traditional Toonie, was called the Shetland Collie. Some breeders tried to bring the size back down by crossing again to toy breeds, but that practice soon ended because those offspring lacked the desired Collie type.

Despite the controversy, many breeders continued the practice of crossing the Shetland dogs with Collies well into the twentieth century, which accounts for the wide variability of sizes found in today's Shelties.

BREED HISTORY IN GREAT BRITAIN

The Kennel Club of Great Britain recognized the little dogs of the islands in 1909, issuing the first registration in March of that year to Badenock Rose, who was designated a Shetland Collie. Many Collie breeders considered the Shetland dogs to be mongrels, however, and protested the name, so beginning in 1914, the dogs were registered as a separate breed known as the Shetland Sheepdog. By 1918, 46 Shelties had appeared in the Stud Book, which records the names of dogs who have produced offspring.

Despite the name change, many considered the Sheltie to be a miniature version of the Rough Collie, and in fact crossed Shelties

Shelties Are Not Miniature Collies

The Shetland Sheepdog is sometimes wrongly called a "miniature Collie." Although the two breeds are related, they have separate histories as modern breeds. They are both believed to trace their ancestries to an older British herding dog who probably resembled the modern Border Collie. On the mainland of Scotland, the older breed gave rise to the modern Collie (Rough and Smooth) and Border Collie. In the more constrained environs of the Shetland Islands, dogs of the older type were crossed with small dogs already on the islands, giving birth to an early version of the Shetland Sheepdog.

with Rough Collies in order to make the head, ears, and coat consistently "Collie-like." Unfortunately, when crossing any two breeds, you cannot choose which genes the pups will inherit and which they will not, and the Collies also contributed larger body size and longer legs. Nevertheless, Sheltie/Collie crosses were not rare, although most were not officially registered with the Kennel Club. More often, breeders referred to the Collie parent as an unregistered Sheltie, or the Sheltie/Collie offspring were not themselves registered but were called unregistered Shelties when their own puppies were registered. In a few cases, purebred Collies may have been fraudulently registered as Shetland Sheepdogs. Around 1915, a new line of dogs emerged that traced its foundation to an unregistered dog called Butcher Boy. This "BB" line still dominates British Sheltie bloodlines.

The restrictions and shortages brought on by World War I put an end to showing and breeding for several years, and to discourage violations of the ban on breeding, dogs born during the war were barred from the show ring for life. In fact, most breeders did not produce puppies under the ban, and by the time the ban was lifted, many Sheltie bloodlines had died out.

BREED HISTORY IN THE UNITED STATES

In 1911, the American Kennel Club (AKC) registered its first Sheltie, Lord Scott, who was imported from the Shetland Islands by John G. Sherman, Jr., of New York. Progress of the breed in the United States was slowed by the World War I breeding ban in

Britain, but when the ban was lifted after the war, imports increased. In 1929, fanciers founded the American Shetland Sheepdog Association (ASSA), which held its first specialty show in 1933.

A few fanciers continued to import dogs from Britain in the 1950s, but most American Shelties trace their pedigrees to dogs imported between the world wars. By the late 1940s, Shelties in the United States and Britain had already diverged, and today they are quite different, making imports rare. This variation is due in part to lack of agreement on the ideal size for the Sheltie. The Kennel Club has long held that the ideal heights for Shelties are 14 inches (36 cm) for bitches (females) and 14.5 inches (37 cm) for dogs (males). The American breed standard adopted in the 1950s defines the correct Sheltie as being between 13 and 16 inches (33 and 41 cm). In general, American Shelties are bigger than British Shelties.

DOGS AND PEOPLE WHO INFLUENCED THE BREED

One of the first Shelties to be registered in Britain was Inverness Yarrow, who sired Kilravock Laddie, the first Shetland Sheepdog to appear in the Kennel Club Stud Book. Kilravock Laddie in turn sired UK Champion Walesby Select, who was imported to the

Knowing a bit about the history and purpose of the early Shetland Sheepdog will give you some insight into your own Sheltie's physical, mental, and behavioral traits.

Kennel Clubs

The American Kennel Club

The American Kennel Club (AKC) is the largest and best-known dog registry in the United States. The AKC maintains registration records for more than a hundred breeds of dogs, including the Shetland Sheepdog, and offers information on many aspects of dog ownership. The AKC also sanctions competition programs in many canine sports, including several in which Shelties excel: obedience, agility, rally, herding, tracking, and conformation.

American Kennel Club
5580 Centerview Drive
Suite 200
Raleigh, NC 27606
(919) 233-9767
www.akc.org
info@akc.org

The United Kennel Club

The United Kennel Club (UKC) is the second largest dog registry in the United States. The UKC maintains registration records for more than a hundred breeds of dogs, including the Shetland Sheepdog, and sanctions competition programs in many canine sports, including obedience, agility, and conformation, sports in which Shelties excel.

The United Kennel Club
100 East Kilgore Road
Kalamazoo, Michigan 490015593
(616) 343-9020

The Kennel Club

The Kennel Club (KC) of Great Britain maintains a registry for dogs in Britain and sanctions competitive events.

The Kennel Club
1 Clarges Street
London W1J 8AB
0870 606 6750
www.the-kennel-club.org.uk

United States. Another Kilravock Laddie son, Pedro, sired Farburn Dinnah (sometimes spelled Dinah) and Hailes Princess, both influential dams.

British Sheltie breeder Miss E.P. Humphries was one of the few people who continued to breed and register dogs during World War I. In 1918, she bred a Sheltie named Wallace to Teena, who was described as an 18-inch (46 cm) golden sable Collie with white markings and prick ears. This controversial cross produced War Baby of Mountfort. Teena was also bred to a Wallace son, Rip of Mountfort, by J.G. Saunders, producing four bitches: Tiny Teena of

Mountfort, Silverlining, KoKo, and Printfield Bess. War Baby and the four bitches profoundly influenced the pedigrees of modern Shelties, particularly in Britain.

English Champion Blaeberry of Clerwood sired Champion Wee Laird O'Downfield, who appears in approximately one-fourth of modern American Sheltie pedigrees, as well as three highly influential bitches: Champion Ashbank Fairy, Natalie of Clerwood, and Downfield Grethe. Close behind in their influence on American Sheltie lines is Champion Peabody Pan, who traced his own pedigree to many of the early greats, including War Baby of Mountfort, Tiny Teena of Mountfort, Printfield Bess, and KoKo.

Another very influential sire of the early era of registrations was Lerwick Jarl, an unregistered black-and-white dog whose descendants included many champions in Britain and Canada. Many of his descendants were tricolors (black, white, and tab) or bi-blacks (black and white), and his genes are still present in many modern Shelties. His full brother, Champion Lerwick Rex, was the first United States champion.

Nearly all American and some British Shelties also trace their lines to Chestnut Rainbow, the unregistered tricolor son of two registered Shelties. He sired a number of important Shelties used to establish American lines, and most modern Shelties in the United States get about 25 percent of their genes from him. Among his most influential offspring were his sons Chestnut Bud, Chestnut Lucky Boy, Redbraes Rollo, and Nut of Houghton Hill, and his daughters Eng. Champion Redbraes Magda, Chestnut Blossom, and Chestnut Garland.

CHARACTERISTICS

of the Shetland Sheepdog

The well-bred Shetland Sheepdog is without a doubt one of the most beautiful of dogs. He is at once athletic and elegant. He moves like a dancer and is clad in a lush coat with a thick mane that sets off his shapely head and sweet, intelligent expression. When viewed in silhouette, the Sheltie appears symmetrical and well-proportioned. The back from the withers to the base of the tail should be relatively short, although the body from the shoulder joint to the rear of the pelvic bone should be moderately long. Dogs (males) should look masculine, and bitches (females) should look feminine. Regardless of sex, the Sheltie is sensitive, gentle, alert, active, agile, and extremely intelligent.

STANDARDS OF PERFECTION

The physical and behavioral traits of the Shetland Sheepdog developed as breeders selected and bred those dogs most capable of performing their assigned jobs. Many generations of selective breeding are necessary to develop a breed, and once it is established, breeders must select their breeding animals very carefully if they want to continue to perpetuate those traits and talents.

To remain true to the breed's origins, breeders use the breed standard, a document that defines the physical, mental, and behavioral characteristics of the ideal Sheltie, to make up the breed's "type." Many traits, such as size, coat quality, and movement, are based on the breed's original or present-day function. Other traits, including preferences for certain markings, are more cosmetic. As a whole, the traits defined by the breed standard make the breed distinct from all others. The breed standard also identifies traits that are allowed but not ideal, and traits that are considered detrimental to the breed and therefore disqualify a dog from competition in conformation shows and from responsible breeding. No individual dog is perfect, but the breed standard provides a sketch of the ideal to which responsible breeders strive.

Pet Shelties produced without regard to the breed standard vary enough that they almost seem to be other breeds. Many are finely built and dainty—they "lack substance," in the jargon—and they often have foxy faces and prick ears. Others have heavy bones, with long,

The Breed Standard

A breed standard is a document that defines the ideal physical, mental, and behavioral characteristics of a particular breed of animal. It describes the traits that good breeders strive to produce, traits that are acceptable but not desirable (minor faults), traits that are considered detrimental to the breed (major faults), and traits that eliminate the animal from competition in conformation shows (disqualifying faults).

broad heads, heavy ears, long necks, or long backs. These dogs can be great, loving pets, but the lack of consistency does mean that any two of them may look and act very different from one another and from Shelties bred for the traits specified by the breed clubs.

Shetland Sheepdog breed standards have been established by the American Kennel Club (AKC), the Kennel Club (KC), and other registries worldwide. The two standards agree, naturally, on many points, although there are some differences between the two. You can read the complete AKC and Kennel Club standards by visiting the organizations' websites at www.akc.org and www.the-kennel-club.org.uk respectively.

The AKC standard begins with a brief history of the breed to help you understand how the physical traits, behavior, and personality of the typical Sheltie enhance his ability to do the job for which he was originally intended. Although he shares many characteristics with the other "collie-type breeds," including the Rough and Smooth Collies and the Border Collie, the Shetland Sheepdog is also distinctive in many ways.

SIZE AND SUBSTANCE

The most obvious difference between the Sheltie and his Collie cousins is size. Like many other breeds of animal developed in the tough environment of the Shetland Islands, the Sheltie is smaller than his counterparts from other parts of Britain. The well-bred Sheltie is not, however, slight of bone. In fact, if we adjust for height, he is a heavier-boned dog than the modern Collie.

The AKC breed standard states that the show Sheltie must stand 13 to 16 inches (33 and 41 cm) at the withers (the high point where the shoulder blades meet). The Kennel Club standard splits the difference, stating that the ideal height is 14.5 inches (37 cm) for dogs (males) and 14 inches (36 cm) for bitches. In the general population, though, the range of sizes is much wider because the breeds used to create the modern Shetland Sheepdog ran the gamut from toys to full-sized Collies. Responsible breeders breed only animals who adhere to the breed standard, but because of the diversity of genes in the breed, even two standard-sized Shelties can produce puppies who mature at up to 20 inches (51 cm) or, less often, under 13 inches (33 cm). Although this range in size can be confusing for the buyer, the fact is that there is only one "Sheltie," and ads for "toy Shelties" or "miniature Collies" are the mark of an ignorant or unscrupulous puppy seller, not a responsible breeder.

If you are planning to buy a Sheltie puppy, you can increase the likelihood that he will mature to within or close to the breed standard if you buy from a responsible breeder who knows her dogs' lines and carefully matches sires (daddy dogs) and dams (mama dogs) who fall within the standard size range. Some puppies may mature a bit outside the standard, but the variation will probably not be extreme. On the other hand, people with little understanding of genetics often produce very small or (more often) very large dogs (as well as more serious problems) by breeding animals that do not adhere to the standard themselves.

If your Sheltie is larger or smaller than the breed standard specifies, don't worry—his size won't affect his health or

Traditionally bred as a working farm dog, the Shetland Sheepdog is agile, sturdy, and well proportioned.

temperament, it won't keep him from participating in performance sports or other activities, and it won't affect his ability to love you and be a terrific companion.

FORM FOLLOWS FUNCTION

The physical traits specified by the breed standard are not just arbitrary measures of beauty. They work together to enhance the dog's ability to perform his traditional jobs as a working farm dog and, today, his new jobs as a canine athlete and healthy companion. There is, of course, some leeway in pets, but the further an individual dog deviates from the breed standard, the less likely it is that he will be able to perform at high levels. In some cases, poor conformation can contribute to the potential for injuries and long-term health problems as well.

Head

The Sheltie's head should be a long, blunt wedge, tapering from the ears to the nose when seen from the top or side. It should show a definite stop, the change in planes where the muzzle meets the skull. If you measure from an imaginary line linking the inner corners of the eyes, the skull and the muzzle should be the same length. The top of the skull should be flat and moderately wide between the ears, and it should be parallel to the top of the muzzle. The cheeks should be flat and should blend smoothly into the muzzle. The jaws should be strong, properly aligned, and well-developed, with a rounded chin and tight lips that meet all around the mouth. The teeth should be properly aligned and should meet in a scissors

Good Breeding Practices

The breed standard is one of the breeder's best tools for producing healthy dogs with the physical and mental traits that make us choose a specific breed. As a buyer, you should know enough about responsible breeding practices to recognize a poor breeder when you meet one. For instance, if you want your Sheltie to grow up to be within or near the standard size range of 13 to 16 inches (33 to 41 cm), you want to know that his parents are within that standard range as well. Genes contributed by the parents do not blend like chocolate syrup and milk, so you can't average out faults. If you breed an oversized Sheltie to an undersized Sheltie, you will get a litter of over- and undersized Shelties. (Just as in human beings, a brown-eyed parent and blue-eyed parent don't have kids with "blue-brown" eyes.)

bite, meaning that the upper incisors and canines fit just in front of their lower counterparts. Ideally, the dog will have no genetically missing teeth.

Eyes and Ears

The Sheltie's eyes and ears are critical players in giving him that distinctively alert and intelligent expression that people find so appealing. According to the breed standard, the eyes are medium in size in relation to the head. The rims are black and almond-shaped rather than round, and the eye openings are set obliquely. The irises must be dark brown except in blue merles, who may have blue eyes, or a combination of blue and brown.

The ears are small and flexible and placed high on top of the skull. When the Sheltie is alert, his ears should stand three-fourths erect, facing forward, with the upper quarter tipping forward. When he's relaxed, his ears should fold lengthwise and lie back. Many Shelties have fully erect ears, and people who intend to show their dogs in conformation often train the tips of the ears to bend forward by taping or gluing them into position as the pup is growing. Getting the fold of the ears correct can be tricky, though, so find someone who is experienced with show Shelties to help you do it properly.

When Talkin' Dogs

In general conversation, the term "dog" is used to mean any domestic canine. Among serious fanciers (and in show catalogs and other documents), however, a male is called a dog and a female is properly called a bitch (in much the same way a female equine is called a mare, or a female pig is called a sow).

Neck, Topline, and Body

The Sheltie's neck should be muscular and arched, and long enough to let him hold his head proudly, as well he might. His back should be muscular and level when he stands on level ground, with a slight arch over the loins (the area between the ribs and pelvis) and a gradual slope over the croup (the area between the pelvic bone and tail). His chest should be deep, reaching to his elbows. The upper portion of his ribs needs to be "well sprung," or nicely rounded, to provide space for his athletic lungs and heart, but the lower part of the ribs should be flattened so that his shoulder and foreleg can move easily alongside the rib cage. His abdomen should rise slightly behind the rib cage but not severely like a Greyhound's. When viewed from the side, the Sheltie's body should appear slightly longer than tall. If you hold his beautiful plume of a tail down along his back legs, it should reach to his hock joints (the joints above the hocks, the long bones above the feet on the hind legs). When he is alert, the Sheltie should hold his tail level with or slightly higher than his back, but never curved forward.

Forequarters and Hindquarters

The breed standard identifies ideal structural features in the Sheltie's forequarters and hindquarters, all meant to facilitate quick, safe movement when the dog is working or playing. Aside from the angles and other specific points, it says that the forelegs and hocks should be straight and muscular, and the joints that move them strong and flexible. The dewclaws—those funny little toes and nails on the inside of the legs above the foot—should be removed from the back legs (if they are present; most Shelties are born without hind dewclaws) and may be removed from the front. The feet themselves should be oval in shape, with arched toes held close together. The pads should be thick and tough, the nails hard, and the feet should point straight ahead when the dog is standing or moving in a straight line.

All these structural qualities enable the Shetland Sheepdog to move quickly and smoothly, with power or "drive" coming from the rear and pushing the dog forward. Although the Sheltie may

The Shetland Sheepdog is most admired for his lush, long coat and the thick mane that sets off his shapely head and sweet, intelligent expression.

prance happily in circles when the biscuit bag opens, when he's trotting, he should lift his feet just high enough to clear the ground. When he walks, his front and rear legs should appear nearly perpendicular to the ground when seen from in front or behind. As his speed increases at a trot, his legs should angle inward toward an imaginary center line until, and at a fast trot, his paw prints should fall in two parallel lines that almost touch.

CLOTHED IN ELEGANCE

Probably the first thing that most people notice about the well-cared-for Shetland Sheepdog is his gorgeous coat. Like many other breeds designed to work outdoors in harsh weather, the Sheltie's body is clothed in a double coat consisting of an outer coat over an undercoat. The long, straight hair of the outer coat is rather harsh in texture and is designed to protect the dog from the elements. Beneath the outer coat lies the undercoat, made up of short, dense, downy hair that insulates the body and causes the outer coat to stand away and look fluffy. The hair around the neck and on the chest is long and thick, particularly in males. The hair on the dog's face, ear tips, and feet is short and smooth, but the backs of the front and hind legs are feathered with long, thick hair. The Sheltie's expressive plume of a tail is also covered with thick, long hair. When Shelties are shown in conformation, they are groomed to enhance the "big hair" look, although excess or straggly hairs on the ears, feet, and hocks are trimmed and tidied. Your pet Sheltie needn't be treated to the show armory of grooming products and tools, but should be groomed regularly both to make his look as good as possible and to keep his skin and coat healthy. (See also Chapter 5 for more on grooming.)

Standard Colors

When you look at a group of Shelties, you may think they come in many colors. But, in fact, the breed standard allows for only three colors, although other colors do occur. In addition, the appearances of individual dogs are modified by the presence or absence of white and tan markings, creating a wide spectrum of individual appearances. Let's start with the basic colors, and then look at Sheltie markings.

Balance

If you attend canine competitions, especially conformation shows, you may hear about "balanced" dogs. Balance refers to structural proportions — especially the appearance and relative proportions of the parts of the head, head-to-body, and height-to-length — that help enable the dog to perform his job. Balance may also refer to approximately equal angles of the joints between the long bones in the front and hind legs.

Sable

The sable coat is the one most people envision when thinking of the Shetland Sheepdog. Sable refers to tan or brown coats ranging from pale yellowish or reddish tan to rich mahogany. Many sables have a reddish cast that some refer to as "red sable." Many sable Shelties, especially the darker ones, have black guard hairs over the brown coat; they are known as "shaded sables" or "tri-factored sables." Regardless of the shade of brown or the presence or absence of black shading or white markings, all brown Shelties are registered as sables.

Black

Black Shelties have black hair over their bodies. For the show ring, the color should be true, rich black. Some black Shelties acquire a reddish cast, called "rusting," which may be inherited, or may be caused by exposure to sun. Rusting has no effect on the dog's health or personality, so it is not a problem for pets or for Shelties in performance sports. A black Sheltie with white and tan markings on the face and legs is called a tri-color. A black Sheltie with white markings but no tan is called a bi-black. A black Sheltie with tan markings but no white at all is called a black and tan.

Merle

Blue merle is ideally a clear silver-blue, often broken

Shedding Facts

The Shetland Sheepdog's trademark glorious coat doesn't come without some effort on your part. Although his genes provide the raw material, your Sheltie's coat — and his home — will soon be a hairy mess without regular grooming.

During most of the year, your Sheltie needs at least one thorough brushing every single week to keep his coat and skin clean and healthy, although two or more brushing sessions per week would be better. Without frequent grooming, his coat will develop mats that can harbor dirt, debris, and moisture, which can potentially lead to skin injuries or infections. Regular brushing also removes dead hair, which helps to reduce the amount that ends up on carpets, furniture, and clothing.

What about shedding, you ask? Shelties shed. And shed. Lots. Dogs who live indoors under artificial light shed a bit all year long. There are times, however, when the Sheltie molts, or "blows," mounds of hair. Spring is the heaviest molting season because this is when he sheds his heavy winter coat, but most dogs also shed in the fall before their new winter coats grow in. Hormonal changes also cause unspayed females to blow their coats after every heat cycle and after weaning puppies. Daily brushing is essential during periods of heavy shedding, both for the sake of your dog and your home.

up by patches of black in varying amounts. Some blue merles have a rusty tinge that is considered undesirable in a show dog but, as with rusty blacks, it has no negative effects on the dog's health or personality. Blue merles are genetically black, but the merle gene dilutes the black color, resulting in a mottled pattern of black and silver. Occasionally, the color dilution occurs without mottling, creating a "self blue," which looks like faded black and which is considered a fault in Shetland Sheepdogs. A blue merle may have tan and white markings, or white only (making him a "bi-blue").

Sable merle is an unusual color pattern that occurs when a puppy inherits the genes for the sable color as well as the genes for merle dilution of the color. Although the breed standard does not specifically disallow sable merle, it does penalize "washed-out or degenerate colors, such as pale sable and faded blue," so sable merles generally do not fare well in the conformation ring.

Sable and black Shelties should have very dark brown eyes. Blue merles may have brown or blue eyes, or one of each, or even "merle" eyes in which brown and blue both appear within one iris. Although genetic eye problems do occur in Shelties (see Chapter 8), they are not related to eye color per se, and dogs with blue or partially blue eyes are no more or less likely to experience vision problems than their brown-eyed brethren.

No matter what color coat an individual Sheltie has, his nose, lips, and eye rims should be black.

Markings

Although an individual may have a coat of a single color with no markings—referred to as "self coloring"—most Shelties in fact have markings that contrast with the main coat color. White markings are common, acceptable, and even desirable in the following places:

- a blaze of white on the forehead, between but not touching the eyes, down the nose, and/or on the sides of the muzzle and the lower jaw
- a full or partial collar of white around the neck
- a bib of white on the chest (ruff)
- on the front legs
- on the hind legs up to the hocks
- on the tip of tail

All or some white markings are preferred (except on black and tan), but absence of these markings is not to be penalized. Patches of white on the body are highly undesirable.

Black and blue merle Shelties can also have tan markings, with or without white.

What About White Shelties?

As discussed, most Shelties have white markings on their heads, necks, chests, legs, and tails. Some individuals, though, have coats that are partially or almost completely white. Although a white Sheltie may be beautiful to look at, not all white dogs are created genetically equal. In fact, two completely different combinations of genes cause white body hair in Shelties, and in some cases nonstandard white fur is also linked to health problems. (See also "Do Merle Shelties Have Special Problems?" in this chapter and "Deafness" in Chapter 8.)

The Sheltie coat can be black, blue merle, or sable, modified by the presence or absence of white and tan markings.

Many Shelties with white on their bodies have no health problems and are fine pets and performance dogs. Unfortunately, in most cases you cannot tell which genes an individual has just by looking at him, which is one reason that full-body white, or white

Do Merle Shelties Have Special Problems?

Merle coloring occurs in many breeds and mixed breeds, including the Shetland Sheepdog. The gene that produces merle coloring works by diluting the dog's base color, so a blue merle Sheltie is genetically a black dog under that beautiful silvery blue or gray coat. Similarly, a sable merle is a sable dog whose color is diluted by the merle gene. Some merle dogs have coats that are primarily the silvery dilute color, while others have large areas of black interspersed with gray (or dilute black). A dog who is genetically a merle but who has barely any merle coloring—maybe a tiny, hard-to-find patch—is called a cryptic merle.

Puppies inherit one gene for each trait from each of their parents. The merle gene is dominant over the solid, or nonmerle, meaning that a dog who inherits a merle gene from at least one parent will be a merle. A heterozygous merle has inherited only one merle gene from one of his parents, and one nonmerle (solid color) gene from the other parent. A heterozygous merle has one merle and one nonmerle gene, and can pass on one or the other of those color options to each of his or her puppies. A dog who inherits two merle genes, one from each parent, is a homozygous ("double") merle. Homozygous merles can occur only when both parents are merles. Statistically, 25 percent—one in four—puppies from two heterozygous merle parents will be homozygous merles. In other words, each puppy from a mating of two heterozygous merles has a 1 out of 4 chance of inheriting two merle genes, one from each parent. Statistics work only over large numbers of litters and puppies, not single litters, so it would be possible to breed two merle parents and get a litter in which all the puppies, or none of the puppies, are merles.

Heterozygous merle dogs have no more risk of inherited problems than do nonmerle dogs with similar ancestry. Homozygous merles, however, often suffer physical problems specifically associated with the presence of two merle dilution genes. The embryonic cells that eventually develop into eyes begin in the same place that color begins, and they may be damaged when two merle genes are present, causing a condition known as merle ocular dysgenesis that may include various malformations of the eye that impair vision in varying degrees. (The other organs develop elsewhere and are not affected by the merle genes.) Homozygous merles are also often partially or completely deaf.

Homozygous merles are usually white over large parts of their bodies and heads, but not all predominantly white Shelties are homozygous merles. The genes that create white markings on the head, chest, legs, and tail tip sometimes extend beyond those areas, so it is possible for a normal, healthy heterozygous merle, or even a nonmerle, to have a lot of white fur. Because lack of pigment in the ear affects the transmission of sound, such a dog may be deaf. However, he will not suffer from the vision problems that affect homozygous merles.

How can you tell whether your merle dog is homozygous? If only one of the parents is a merle, then their merle puppies must be heterozygous (because the nonmerle parent has only nonmerle genes to pass on). If you don't know about the parents, the only ways to tell whether a merle dog is homozygous or heterozygous is either to have a genetic profile done or to identify obvious signs of merle ocular dysgenesis.

over more than half of the dog's body, is severely penalized in the show ring and is considered undesirable for breeding purposes. Let's look at the two types of white Shelties.

One type of body white is caused by the same genes that create standard white markings, often referred to as an "Irish" or "Dutch" pattern of markings. Among Sheltie fanciers, such dogs are said to be "white factored." In some dogs, the genes that determine the size and placement of the white markings extend their influence beyond those areas specified in the breed standard.

The result is white "markings" that reach up the legs and over the haunches, over the entire tail, and from the neck and chest across the back and sides. In extreme cases, the body may be completely white or have only small patches of color. The heads of these dogs, though, are colored like any other Sheltie's head, which is why they are called "color-headed whites." In Collies, color-headed whites are allowed in the show ring, and some Sheltie fanciers believe the penalty for white on the body should be removed from the Sheltie breed standard as well. Whether or not they are welcome in the conformation ring, color-headed whites have no more health problems than any standard-color Sheltie; they are wonderful companions and can compete in all canine performance sports.

The other type of white Sheltie is the homozygous, or double, merle, which can result from breeding a merle bitch to a merle dog. Most homozygous merles have a lot of white on their heads as well as their bodies, although some do not. The "double dilution" caused by the presence of two merle genes often causes vision and/or hearing problems.

How do you know for sure whether a white Sheltie is a color-headed white or a homozygous merle? First, if possible, look at the parents' color and markings. If either the dam (mother) or sire (father) is black or sable, the puppies cannot be homozygous merle because a nonmerle parent has no merle genes to contribute to the offspring. If both parents are merles, a white pup may be homozygous merle, but not necessarily. If you know that the parents are both merles, or if you don't know about the parents, then look to the traits present in the dog himself. If his head is colored with only a white blaze and possibly white muzzle, he is probably a color-headed white. If there is white other than a blaze on the head and ears, he is most likely a homozygous merle. In that case, you may want to have his hearing tested. Some, but not all, of the eye problems associated with doubling the merle gene are often obvious—the pupil may be off-center and/or oddly shaped, for instance.

TEMPERAMENT AND BEHAVIOR

The Sheltie's personality endears him to his fans at least as much as does his beauty. But make no mistake—some of his behavioral traits also make him completely unsuitable for some people.

As with any breed, one person's dream dog is another's canine catastrophe. By the same token, the perfect home for one dog may be a terrible place for another.

Before we delve into the particulars of typical Sheltie temperament and behavior, here's a small caveat: no two dogs are exactly alike. Within any breed, typical traits occur on a continuum. Even within a single litter, individual puppies may vary greatly in their attitudes, intelligence, energy level, and so on (just as children within a human family vary). That's why, if you are looking for a dog, it's important to be clear about the traits you want to be strong in your own Sheltie, and those you would prefer to minimize. As we'll see in the next chapter, if you know what you want in a canine companion, a responsible, knowledgeable breeder or rescuer can help match you with the right Sheltie. Now let's talk about those temperament and personality traits that are considered typical of the Sheltie, the range of variation that is common, and the implications of those traits for people who live with Shelties.

The breed standard describes the Shetland Sheepdog as "intensely loyal, affectionate, and responsive." These traits combine to make the Sheltie a highly trainable dog who is eager to please his special person or people. Shelties are very sensitive, and they respond beautifully to positive, reward-based training methods (see

Intensely loyal and affectionate, the Sheltie is known to be an intelligent and highly trainable dog who is eager to please his special person or family.

Selective Breeding

Conscientious breeders do not allow just any dog and bitch to produce puppies. On the contrary, they study canine genetics and learn as much as possible about individual animals and bloodlines. They also practice selective breeding, using their knowledge to increase the odds that their puppies will have desirable traits and to reduce or eliminate the chances that their puppies will have undesirable traits, including health and temperament problems.

Chapter 6). They are, in fact, one of the top breeds in the sports of obedience, rally, and agility, all of which require a close rapport between dog and handler.

Although Shelties are loving with their own people, most are naturally reserved with strangers; they like to size up new people and animals before interacting with them. It's a rare Sheltie who greets all comers with enthusiastic welcome, so this may not be the best breed for someone who prefers a canine social butterfly. More importantly, Sheltie puppies need to be heavily socialized, especially during critical developmental periods, to prevent lifelong problems (see Chapters 2 and 6). Undersocialized Shelties, and those with inherited temperament extremes, may be painfully shy with new people and animals, and nervous or frightened in new situations.

Most Shelties instinctively guard family, home, and property by barking to alert their owners and to frighten off intruders. In the isolated farms of their native Shetland Islands, this was a useful behavior. In modern suburban or urban life, barking can be annoying and, not uncommonly, can create friction with neighbors. Barking can be controlled to some extent (see Chapter 6), but it is nevertheless a trait to consider before choosing a Sheltie.

Like all herding breeds, the Shetland Sheepdog is a working dog at heart and as such he needs a "job." If he has a flock of sheep to herd, great, but for most modern Shelties, "work" takes the form of canine competitive sports, backyard games with flying disks and tennis balls, and long walks, jogs, or runs with a human partner. Without adequate physical and mental exercise, the Sheltie will write his own job description, which may include rounding up the kids and other pets, barking endlessly, and other annoying "duties."

THE RIGHT DOG IN THE RIGHT PLACE

People often ask whether a Sheltie will fit into their life in a particular environment, such as an apartment, condo, or a big suburban backyard. The truth is that the best place for a Shetland Sheepdog is not a place at all. It's alongside a person or family committed to giving him what he needs to live a healthy, full doggy life: good food, health care, exercise, grooming, training, and, above all, love and affection.

That said, physical environment can make a difference to an individual owner's ability to provide for a Sheltie's needs. Most have lots of energy, especially when they are young, and they need lots of exercise to expend that energy safely. As a Sheltie owner, it's your responsibility to see that your dog gets the exercise he needs on a regular basis. If you don't have a yard where you can safely play running games with your dog, you'll need to take him for long walks every single day. On the other hand, if you have a house with a safely fenced yard, you can't just send your Sheltie out the door and expect him to exercise. He wants a playmate, and unless you have other dogs who will romp along with him, you need to go out and play together. But that's half the fun of living with a Sheltie!

When I say "living with a Sheltie," I mean exactly that. Shelties thrive as indoor companions and should never be banished to a backyard, basement, or other isolated place. Dogs are social animals, and they need the companionship of people as well as other animals. Not only is it cruel to sentence a pet to isolation, but loneliness often leads to a variety of unwanted behaviors, including destructive digging or chewing, neurotic behaviors, and barking.

SHELTIES AND CHILDREN

Shetland Sheepdogs can be superb family dogs. Their size and their affectionate, playful nature make them potentially ideal companions for many children. For a child who is interested in participating in a 4-H dog club or in junior showmanship or other competitive canine sports, the Sheltie's willingness to learn and perform make him an ideal teammate.

It's vital to remember, though, that good kid–dog relationships aren't automatic. Children must be taught to respect dogs and treat them with gentle kindness. Dogs must be trained to respect children as well. Children, especially when very young, can inadvertently hurt a dog, and even the most patient canine may try to defend himself. Dogs discipline their wayward puppies with nips and grips, and it's

Keeping Kids and Dogs Safe

Teach your child these basic rules for interacting safely with your Sheltie and other dogs:

- Don't run up to a dog—walk.

- Don't scream or yell around dogs—speak in a normal voice. Never pretend to bark or growl at a dog.

- Some dogs are afraid of strangers or don't like to be petted. Always ask for permission before you try to pet a dog you don't know. If the owner says it's okay, then approach the dog calmly and quietly.

- Always let the dog sniff your open hand before you try to pet him, even if he knows you.

- Don't reach over a dog's head until after he has a chance to sniff you. The best place to pet a dog is under his chin or on his chest.

- Don't touch a dog who doesn't know you're there—he might snap just because he's startled. If he's sleeping, leave him alone. If he just doesn't see you, talk to him in a normal voice to get his attention.

- If a dog tries to get away from you, don't grab or chase him. If you frighten him, he might bite.

- If you see a dog without a person, don't approach him.

- Don't tease dogs. Teasing is mean and may frighten or anger the dog.

- Don't try to take food, toys, bones, or anything else away from a dog. If the dog (even your own dog) has something he shouldn't have, ask an adult to help.

- Don't bother a dog who is eating, sleeping, going potty, or taking care of puppies.

- Don't stare at a dog's eyes, especially if the dog doesn't know you.

- If you're running and a dog chases you, stop, stand still, and be quiet. If the dog comes close to you, "be a tree"—cross your arms with your hands on your shoulders and don't look at the dog.

- If a dog barks, growls, or shows you his teeth, he's warning you to leave him alone. If you see a dog acting like that, look away from the dog's face and walk very slowly sideways until the dog relaxes or you're out of sight.

- If a dog attacks you, "be a ball"—get down on your knees, and curl up with your face tucked into your legs and your arms around your head. Lie still and don't move or scream.

- If a dog bites you, tell an adult right away. If you don't know the dog, try to remember where you were when he bit you, what the dog looked like, where the dog lives or which way he went after he bit you, and who else saw him bite you.

- If you see dogs fighting, stay away from them and find an adult to help.

unfair and unrealistic to expect your Sheltie to understand that his instinctive parenting techniques are not allowed with human babies and toddlers. A responsible adult should always be present, alert, and in a position to intervene whenever young children interact with dogs.

SHELTIES AND OTHER PETS

Most Shelties get along well with other pets. Because of their relatively small size, some care should be taken when they interact with large dogs, especially those you don't know. Not all dogs are friendly, and even a friendly big galoot can cause devastating injuries.

Many Shelties are great friends with cats, too, but initial introductions should be controlled and cautious. Some Shelties are prone to chasing and even attacking cats, and some cats will bite and claw dogs, especially if they are frightened. For safety, keep your dog on a leash around your cat at first, and be sure your cat always has an escape route and a safety zone that your dog can't get to. Given time, most Shelties and cats will learn to at least tolerate one another.

Smaller pets, like rabbits and rodents, as well as birds, should always be protected from your Sheltie. Dogs are predators, after all, and little furry creatures are prey. Friendships do sometimes develop, and some dogs are gentle and trustworthy with even the tiniest family members, but the instinct to chase and kill can be overpowering. Caution is always the best policy.

Most Shelties get along well with other pets when raised together.

Chapter

3

PREPARING

for Your Shetland Sheepdog

Y ou've done your homework, and you understand that Shelties, like all pets, bring challenges as well as joys to their owners. You know that, in addition to being your beautiful companion, a Sheltie will shed, require considerable exercise and grooming, bark quite a bit, and otherwise put demands on your time and budget. Like many of the breed's fanciers, you've decided that a Sheltie is worth the effort and will suit your personality and lifestyle. Are you finished making decisions? Not yet! In fact, now you get down to the nitty-gritty of finding your own Shetland Sheepdog. You'll need to explore specific options regarding your preferences for a puppy or an adult dog; whether you prefer a male or female; whether you will want a pet, performance, or show dog, etc. You'll also need to know what to ask when buying or adopting a Sheltie, and what you can do to make the transition to Sheltie owner go as smoothly as possible.

Although certain traits are common to Shetland Sheepdogs as a breed, each individual inherits those traits in unique amounts and combinations. In other words, dogs are not interchangeable, even within a breed. So, before you go looking for your ideal Sheltie buddy, think about what you want from your dog and what your dog can expect from you.

PUPPY OR ADULT?

Many people automatically think "puppy" when they look for a new canine companion. There's certainly nothing cuter than a baby Sheltie, and if you have the time and energy to devote to a young dog's developmental needs, a puppy and you may be right for one another. Bringing home a puppy has a downside, though. If you've never raised a dog, or if it's been a long time since you did, consider this serious commitment carefully before you buy or adopt one.

Young puppies are a lot like human babies. A puppy will need to potty in the wee hours of the morning. He may cry for the first few nights—after all, he's used to sleeping with his mother and siblings. A Sheltie puppy will need lots of daily exercise, and he'll need to be supervised at all times to keep him—and your belongings—safe. Although Shelties are usually easy to housetrain, your puppy will undoubtedly have a few accidents in your

Many considerations go into selecting the right dog for you and your family. Choose an adult if you do not have the time and energy to devote to puppy rearing.

home while he is learning. Then, before you know it, your baby dog will be an adolescent. He'll be packed with energy and will need training and activities to challenge his mind as well as his body.

Another very important and time-consuming aspect of raising Shelties properly is their need for socialization. The breed's natural tendency to be reserved with strangers can lead to lifelong shyness and fearfulness without proper handling, especially during the first four months. (See Chapter 6 for a detailed discussion of the socialization process.) The opportunity for socializing a puppy is fairly short, and for many people, choosing a mature Sheltie (two years old or older) who is past this critical socialization period may be a better choice.

Keep in mind that puppies don't always grow up to be quite what we picture. Many people think that by getting a young puppy they can determine the adult dog's personality, but that's true only to a limited extent. A puppy's genetic makeup is determined at conception, and it has a strong bearing on not only his looks but also on his temperament, personality, intelligence, and behavior. Proper upbringing can enhance the good, and possibly subdue some less desirable traits, but a knowledgeable breeder can help you choose a puppy who is likely to become the dog you hope for, although no one knows for sure how a particular puppy will mature.

On the other hand, when you choose an adult Sheltie from a rescue organization, shelter, or breeder, what you see is pretty much what you get. Many dogs become more confident and improve physically with better food, care, and training, but the essential dog is already apparent. Some people are afraid that an adult won't bond to a new person or family, but in fact most adult Shelties can and do so very quickly. Some terrific older puppies and adults are available from Shetland Sheepdog rescue organizations, and breeders will sometimes offer retired show dogs to pet homes for a nominal fee after having them altered.

If you have the time and inclination to raise a puppy properly, the process can be very rewarding. But if the work of raising a puppy seems overwhelming, don't be afraid to adopt an adult.

SHELTIE BOY OR SHELTIE GIRL?

Many people have a strong opinion about which sex makes a better companion. The truth is that the individual's personality is far more important than his or her sex, especially if the dog is altered.

Other than heredity, training, and socialization, the strongest influence on your Shetland Sheepdog's behavior is his or her reproductive status. In both males and females, the hormones that

Do You Really Want a Sheltie?

The Shetland Sheepdog is generally a healthy, even-tempered, and obedient companion, but he is not right for everyone. Although there are individual variations, the following traits are nearly universal:

- Shelties are loud, enthusiastic barkers, especially in groups.
- Shelties shed heavily and are prone to tangles and mats. Frequent brushing and vacuuming are a way of life for owners.
- Shelties are extremely loyal to one person or family, but reserved with strangers. Your Sheltie will not buddy up to all your friends and family.
- Shelties are sensitive and react negatively to loud or sharp noises.
- Shelties have a strong prey drive and will chase anything that moves, so they must always be fenced or on a leash when outdoors.
- Shelties need plenty of daily exercise to use up their energy, and a "job" or activity to exercise their minds as well as their bodies.
- Shelties want to be with their people and are very sensitive to their moods and actions. They should not be left alone for long periods, and they should be handled and trained with love and gentleness.

drive reproduction exert a powerful influence not only on a dog's urge to mate, but also on many other behaviors. Sexually intact Shelties of both sexes are much more likely to mark their territories with urine, indoors and out. They are more prone to wander away in search of romance, behave aggressively with people and other dogs, and indulge in other annoying sex-based behaviors.

If you want a stable, affectionate, devoted pet, look for a Sheltie with a sound temperament and a personality you like. Then socialize and train him or her properly, and have him or her neutered or spayed. If you think you may want to breed Shelties, learn all you can about the breed itself and what responsible breeding practices entail, find a breeder who has healthy Shelties and who is willing to mentor you, and start with the best-quality dog you can find. Plenty of average pets are available, so the only good reason to breed dogs these days is to improve the breed.

PET, PERFORMANCE, OR SHOW DOG?

Another question to ask yourself is, "What do I want from my Sheltie?" Are you looking for a pet whose full-time job is to be your buddy? Do you want a teammate to compete with in conformation, obedience, agility, herding trials, or other sports? Do you want to become a breeder? Knowing what you want from your dog will help you not only to choose your individual Sheltie, but also to choose where he will come from. And having a clear idea of what qualities you are seeking in your dog will help your breeder or rescue volunteer guide your choice or, if you prefer, choose the right dog for you. Although the process of finding the right dog can be complicated (see "Finding Your Shetland Sheepdog"), here are a few general factors to consider.

Temperament should be a critical factor in choosing a Sheltie, and for the pet owner, it is without question the single most important trait in a dog. Too often people become fixated on what a dog looks like, but when you live with a dog, pretty truly is as pretty does.

If you are looking for a competition dog, you still want a sound temperament, of course, but you want more than that. You also want a puppy or dog who strives to be with people (at least one person) and to please them. Proper physical structure is important not only for speed and agility, but for longevity in the sport, because a dog with poor structure will eventually break down

If you want a stable, affectionate, devoted pet, look for a Sheltie with a sound temperament and a personality you like.

under the stress of training and competing. You also may want specific traits that enhance the likelihood a dog will succeed in a particular activity. Problem-solving ability, for instance, is helpful in obedience and herding dogs, and strong food and play drives are helpful in obedience and agility training. If you want to show in the conformation ring, your Sheltie will have to conform closely to the breed standard, and he will have to be trained, groomed, and presented properly.

Do you think you may want to breed Shelties? Responsible breeding is a serious commitment that requires a considerable investment in time, money, and most importantly, love for the breed. The American Shetland Sheepdog Association (ASSA) offers the following recommendations for anyone who plans to breed Shelties:

- study and understand the breed standard
- learn the history of the breed
- learn about the important dogs and bloodlines of the past and present
- join the ASSA and your local ASSA member club, and make use of the educational materials and events they offer
- attend the ASSA National Specialty and local shows to watch, listen, and learn
- learn as much as possible about Sheltie genetics, including inheritance of health problems
- get to know ethical Sheltie breeders and learn from them
- read the ASSA guidelines for ethical behavior

Many breeders are people who first owned and loved a pet Sheltie and then decided they wanted to breed. If you fit that profile, resist the temptation to "practice" with a litter from your pet. Keep loving your dog, but please breed not just to produce a litter but to produce the very best dogs possible.

FINDING YOUR SHETLAND SHEEPDOG

Both nature and nurture affect how your puppy will mature. How you raise him is, of course, important. No less important, though, are his genetic makeup and the care he and his mother receive from his breeder. If you plan to purchase a Sheltie puppy, you're much more likely to get a healthy pup with a sound temperament if you are selective about where you buy him.

The ASSA, other canine organizations, and reproductive veterinarians generally recommend certain tests and practices designed to increase the chances that all puppies will be born healthy and cared for properly to enhance the likelihood that they and their parents will live long, healthy, and happy lives. Unfortunately, some people produce and sell puppies without following these recommendations. Some mean well but are ignorant of responsible breeding practices. Others don't care much about the dogs, just the money they make selling them. The uninformed or unwary buyer may luck out and get a reasonably healthy pup, but the odds are not in their favor. Poorly bred puppies often have serious problems, including vision loss, hip dysplasia, epilepsy, autoimmune disease, shyness, hyperactivity, and aggression—problems that responsible breeders work hard to prevent.

For all these reasons, insist on seeing proof of responsible breeding. Remember, your Sheltie should share your life for the next dozen or more years. It's worth the time and effort to make sure he has been properly handled by someone who truly cares for their dogs. Besides, if you love the breed, you owe it to the dogs to discourage bad breeding by refusing to support it with your dollars. But what exactly should you look for? Let's take a look.

Breeders

Responsible breeders have specific goals in mind when they match a sire (father) and dam (mother). They look for specific traits

Visiting Breeders

When you begin to visit breeders, don't plan back-to-back visits on the same day because it is extremely easy to transfer diseases and parasites to another location, even if the facilities look very clean. Between visits be sure to shower and change into clean clothes, including your shoes.

in each potential parent that complement those of the other. They seek to improve the dogs of each generation, although breeders may define "improvement" differently. Some seek success in the conformation ring. Others breed for quick agility competitors, strong herding dogs, or smart, responsive obedience competitors. Some breed for versatility. All in all, their ultimate goal is to produce the best-quality dogs according to the breed standard.

If you are looking for a Sheltie for a particular activity, look for breeders who participate in it or who have produced puppies who have done well in the activity. If you are looking for a pet, look for breeders who produce healthy pups with the sorts of traits you want to live with. Puppies can vary widely in personality and potential within a litter, so buy your Sheltie from someone who understands your vision of *your* Shetland Sheepdog.

Health Guarantees

Like all living things, Shetland Sheepdogs are potentially at risk for certain health problems, some of which are inherited. Screening tests are available for some of these problems, and responsible breeders follow the recommendations for testing parents and puppies.

A number of tests are recommended for Shelties used for breeding, and in some cases for Sheltie puppies (see "Recommended Health Screenings" as well as Chapter 8 for more information on the inherited diseases themselves). Before you buy a puppy, ask to see written proof that he and his parents have passed these tests. Responsible breeders will not be insulted by your request. In fact, they will be pleased that you have done your homework and care about the welfare of the breed as a whole.

We do not have tests for all inherited diseases, so responsible breeders educate themselves about their dogs' family trees and avoid breeding animals considered to be at high risk. For instance, because there is at present no test to determine whether a dog carries the genes for primary (inherited) epilepsy, it's essential that the breeder know about the incidence of the disease in her dogs' families so that she can avoid high-risk crosses. The same goes for particular diseases of the liver, kidney, pancreas, immune system, and skin, and some cancers. Before you buy a puppy, ask about problems in the bloodline. Anyone who tells you that there are no

Responsible breeders are committed to producing the best-quality dogs according to the breed standard.

problems at all in a particular line is either ignorant or dishonest.

Does this mean that all Shelties have health issues? Not at all. In fact, they are generally healthy, long-lived dogs. But all families (including our own human families) carry the potential for certain problems, so conscientious breeders and smart buyers alike educate themselves and do everything possible to prevent them. And while no one can guarantee that your Sheltie will never have a problem, responsible breeding and buying can make them much less likely.

Quality and Cost: How Much Is That Doggy?

How much will your Sheltie cost, and why are some Shetland Sheepdogs so much more expensive than others? Good questions. First, breeding responsibly is expensive. By the time a breeder buys a high-quality bitch, has her tested for inherited diseases, and pays the costs of breeding her to a high-quality stud dog, she has a lot invested. And that doesn't include the costs of training and showing to demonstrate the bitch's quality and abilities.

You should naturally expect to pay less for a responsibly bred pet Sheltie puppy than for a competition or breeding prospect. Keep in mind, though, that price itself does not ensure quality. Neither do registration papers. (See also "New Dog Paperwork.") As long as there are buyers who will pay good money for puppies without asking to see proof of testing for genetic diseases, there will be sellers willing to sell them. Be a savvy puppy buyer!

Recommended Health Screenings

All living things, including dogs, purebred or mixed, carry genes that potentially contribute to strong, healthy bodies and minds, or to inherited health problems. To minimize the chances that puppies will inherit genetic diseases, the following screening tests are recommended for both parents prior to breeding. Please note: Tests do not yet exist for all potential inherited problems, which is another good reason to work with a knowledgeable, responsible breeder who has researched her dogs' bloodlines and done all she can to breed physically and mentally healthy puppies.

Test/Disease: Thyroid panel to detect autoimmune thyroid disease.

How: Blood evaluation by specialty lab. Full panel is recommended to test for Total T4, Free T4, Total T3, Free T3, T4 autoantibodies, T3 autoantibodies, TSH (thyroid-stimulating hormone), and TgAA. (Simple T4 screening will not detect early signs of thyroid disease.)

When: Every 2 to 3 years. Ask to see the report from the testing laboratory.

Test/Disease: Hip x-rays to detect the presence of hip dysplasia.

How: The hips are x-rayed according to specific guidelines and sent to the screening agency, where orthopedic specialists evaluate them.

When: Four months to two years, depending on the certifying organization. Ask to see the certificate from the Orthopedic Foundation for Animals (OFA), PennHIP, or other appropriate organization.

Test/Disease: Test to detect von Willebrand's Disease (vWD), a bleeding disorder.

How: DNA sample collected by swabbing the inside of the dog's cheek is tested to determine whether the dog has vWD, is a carrier, or is free of the disease. (An older blood test for vWD is no longer considered accurate.)

When: Once, at any time in the dog's life. (If you are purchasing a breeding prospect, ask for the results of testing on puppies you are considering.)

Test/Disease: Eye exams to test for inherited disease, particularly Collie Eye Anomaly (CEA) (sometimes called Sheltie Eye Syndrome, or SES) and Progressive Retinal Atrophy (PRA). (See also Chapter 8.)

How: Examination by a veterinary ophthalmologist.

When: Initially at five to seven weeks of age for CEA. Shelties used for breeding or who are active in sports that require good vision should be reexamined every year or two. Ask to see the examination form filled out by the examining veterinarian, or a CERF certificate. For parents, the test should be dated within 12 months prior to the breeding. Puppies should be tested between 6 to 8 weeks of age.

Price can certainly be a factor in the choice you make, but don't let what seems to be a bargain fool you into buying a poorly bred puppy. You'll nearly always be better off paying more for a dog who has been carefully bred and raised by a responsible breeder. Of course, we all know someone who has gotten a reasonably nice pet from a seller who doesn't follow responsible breeding practices. You might be one of these lucky people, or you might end up with a sickly Sheltie and have to pay many times the cost of a well-bred pup in vet bills.

If you don't want to pay the price for a responsibly bred Shetland Sheepdog, why not adopt a puppy or dog from a rescue group or shelter? You and the dog you provide with a much-needed home will both win, and you won't support irresponsible breeding. Adoption fees for rescued Shelties are generally very reasonable.

The Adoption Option

Many fine adolescent and adult dogs in need of good, loving homes, including Shelties, can always be found in breed rescues, shelters, and pounds. Again, doing your homework and knowing what to ask and what to look for will aid you in selecting and adopting the right dog for you and your family.

Shetland Sheepdog Rescue Programs

Breed rescue programs consist of both groups and individuals who take in and foster homeless animals until they can be placed in suitable new homes. Rescuers are almost always unpaid volunteers who donate their time, dog-handling skills, and love. A national organization, usually dedicated to a specific breed, operates as the hub for regional and local rescue groups who maintain an informative website and offer referrals for potential adopters and for people needing to place Shelties. Many are listed in the AKC

website at www.akc.org.

Why are Shetland Sheepdogs in need of rescue? Some have lost their owners to death or disability, or a serious change in personal or family circumstances. Others were found as strays and efforts to locate their owners have failed. Once in a while, people fail to pick up their dogs from a veterinary office, boarding kennel, or groomer, and rescues sometimes take Shelties confiscated from puppy

A breed rescue or shelter can be a great source if you are looking to acquire an adult Sheltie.

mills, "collectors" who have too many dogs, or abusive owners. Sometimes rescuers have no idea why a dog lost his home.

Although a minority of rescued dogs have serious behavior problems or come from bad situations, most Shelties are turned over to rescue just for being who they are meant to be: intelligent, energetic dogs who shed lots of hair and bark quite a bit. They were often purchased by people who liked the look and size of the breed, but found they couldn't live with the real-life dog. While many of the dogs need some basic obedience training, most have no real behavioral problems that training, exercise, and remedial socialization won't fix.

Most rescued dogs live with foster volunteers while waiting for their new homes. Fostering provides a "normal" setting in which caretakers can assess each dog's temperament, behavior, and level of training. Knowing about each foster dog's individual personality and quirks enables rescuers to match the dog to an appropriate new home. Responsible rescuers spay or neuter intact dogs prior to placement, or they will require adopters to do so within a short time after placement. Each rescued animal is examined by a veterinarian, and potential adopters are advised if problems are found. If a rescued dog needs training, foster caretakers usually begin that process.

If you want to adopt a rescued Sheltie, you will submit an application, provide references, and agree to a home visit. You'll sign an adoption contract agreeing to provide proper care and to return the dog to the organization if you can't keep him. You'll pay an adoption fee, or be asked for a donation. Please be generous. Private support is the lifeblood of rescue programs. And don't forget to send updates to your dog's rescuers occasionally. The rescue volunteer's best reward is knowing that a dog who passed through her hands is thriving and bringing someone joy.

Shelters and Pounds

Shetland Sheepdogs show up in shelters for the same reasons they find their way to rescue. Adopting a dog from a shelter can be highly rewarding, but proceed cautiously. Some shelter workers are very knowledgeable about dogs and good at identifying breeds and mixes, but some are not. If it's important to you that the dog you adopt be a purebred Shetland Sheepdog, take someone who really knows the breed with you to help evaluate candidates.

When you find a dog who you think might be the one for you, ask lots of questions about his known history, how he's been evaluated, who did the evaluation, and what was included. If you are uneasy about the dog's behavior, walk away. If you lack confidence in the shelter personnel's ability to assess the dog and to give you knowledgeable advice, find another shelter or a rescue group. You won't do the dog any favors if you take him home and discover that you can't manage his behavior or emotional baggage.

Vet Checkup

To ensure that your new puppy or adult dog is healthy, have him examined by your vet within 72 hours after bringing him home.

A well-run shelter will be reasonably clean. Dogs awaiting adoption may be thin and in need of a bath, but should look fairly healthy. Be cautious about adopting a dog who appears to be ill, no matter how sorry you feel for him—you don't want to bring home an infectious disease, especially if you already have a dog or your neighbors do. If you want a specific dog but are concerned about his condition, ask if you can have him examined by your own vet. Some shelters will allow this; others will require you to adopt the animal first. If you do adopt a dog with questionable health, take him to your vet for a thorough exam and possible quarantine *before* you take him home. Many problems can be fixed with proper food, exercise, and care, but it would be tragic if your good intentions harmed another dog in your home or neighborhood.

Be aware, too, that dogs in shelters are often lonely, depressed, and frightened. A little time in a quiet place and a few treats may help break the ice. The prospective adoptee should meet your whole family before you decide, but don't overwhelm a nervous dog with a raucous first meeting. Most kids are sympathetic, gentle, and quiet when they understand, but if your children are too young to exercise restraint, think twice about bringing home a very nervous dog, and supervise all interaction until you are absolutely certain that both your dog and your children will treat the other with kindness and respect.

Private Adoptions

People give up their pets to new homes for all sorts of reasons, some of them perfectly legitimate. Be careful, though, if you look into a private adoption, especially if you don't personally know the person and the dog. Some people "forget to mention" serious health or behavioral issues that may be the real reason they are placing the dog. If the problem stems from lack of proper care or training, the dog may be fine in the right home. But some problems, such as a history of biting, are serious, so don't be shy about asking specific questions, including the following:

- Why is this dog being placed?
- Does he get along with other animals?
- When did the dog last have a veterinary exam?
- Has he ever been lame, had allergies, or had seizures?
- Does he take regular heartworm preventive, and when was he last tested for heartworm and other parasites?
- Has this dog ever bitten, snapped, or threatened to bite a person?

Ask to see the dog's veterinary record. If records are unavailable, call the vet who has seen the dog, explain that you are thinking of adopting, and ask if there's anything you need to know. If the dog has no history of veterinary care, ask if you can have the dog examined by your own vet at your expense before you commit to adopting him. Invite the owner along for the ride or ask her to meet you at the vet's office if she won't let you take the dog otherwise. If there's no health care record and you can't have the dog checked out, be alert and cautious, and use your best judgment.

NEW DOG PAPERWORK

When you buy a purebred Sheltie pup who is eligible for registration, be sure that you get the paperwork necessary to transfer official ownership to your name. The specific form you need to submit will vary depending on the age of the dog, the registry (AKC, UKC, KC), and on whether you are getting a puppy who will be registered for the first time or an older dog whose registration you are transferring to your name. Be sure that the seller signs the form as required. If for some reason the paperwork is not available (perhaps it has not yet been sent by the registry), ask the seller for an agreement in writing that specifies when you will receive the paperwork. Remember, though, that registration papers verify only that your Sheltie is registered. They do not indicate the dog's quality, temperament, or health.

To safeguard each puppy's well-being and to protect the financial and emotional investment she has in breeding quality dogs, your breeder may place certain requirements that affect registration on your purchase. For instance, she may insist on retaining co-ownership of the pup until certain conditions are met, or she may withhold the papers on a pet until the dog is spayed or neutered. There is nothing unethical about this, but be sure that you understand all terms of the sale before you buy the puppy. A written contract that spells them out in detail is the best way

Whether you are choosing a puppy or an adult, your first consideration is that the dog appears to be well cared for and healthy.

Signs of a Healthy 7- to 12-Week-Old Puppy

A healthy puppy:

- is solid and well proportioned
- is neither too thin nor potbellied (he may be malnourished or infested with roundworms)
- has soft, glossy fur
- has no red, itchy, or bald spots, and no fleas
- has a clean anal area
- has bright, clear eyes
- has pink gums and healthy breath smelling only of the slightly musky odor of "puppy breath"
- has a correct bite and properly aligned jaws
- has a clean, damp nose with no sign of discharge
- breathes without sneezing, coughing, or wheezing
- has clean ears
- moves well, with no signs of lameness or other problems
- is happy and playful—except when he's asleep

to prevent misunderstandings. It's not a bad idea to show the agreement to both an attorney and an experienced dog person before you complete the purchase.

PICK OF THE LITTER

You've zeroed in on the characteristics you want in your Sheltie, and you've decided where you will get your dog. But how do you decide which Sheltie to bring home?

Whether you are choosing a puppy or an adult dog, your first consideration is that the dog appears to be healthy and well cared for. His body should be solid and well-proportioned, his coat soft and intact, his eyes bright and clear, his nose clean and damp, his gums pink and teeth healthy, and his movement normal.

If you're choosing an adult dog, take the time to find an individual whose personality clicks with your own and one who will fit into your lifestyle. If the first (or second, or third) dog you meet doesn't quite seem to fit the bill, be patient. You and your new canine companion will be much happier if you take the time to find the right match.

If you're buying or adopting a puppy rather than an adult,

choosing may be more difficult, especially if you are relying on the impression you form in a single short meeting. In general, a Sheltie puppy should be playful and alert. He may be reserved at first and cautious about approaching strangers, but once he has checked you out he should be friendly. But if puppies have been playing all afternoon, you may not get an accurate picture of individual personalities; for example, the one you think is calm and quiet may actually be a hooligan who happens to be worn out—which is another good reason to get your Sheltie from a responsible breeder or rescuer who knows each puppy as an individual. Tell the breeder what you want and do not want in a dog, and let her help you select the right pet.

THE BEST TIME TO BRING YOUR PUPPY HOME

Some people think that a puppy must come to his new home at exactly seven weeks of age or he won't bond with his new family. Not true! This "seven-week myth" is based on a misunderstanding of research that showed puppies who don't have positive contact with people—meaning any people at all—by their seventh week will have trouble bonding with humans throughout their lives. In fact, during the short time from the seventh to twelfth weeks of a puppy's life it *is* critical that the pup meet lots of friendly people and animals if he's to develop proper social skills, but the people he meets do *not* have to be the ones with whom he'll spend his life. In fact, many puppies benefit from staying with their mothers and siblings until they are nine to twelve weeks old or older. Puppies younger than seven weeks should not be taken from their mothers and siblings (unless, of course, the environment poses a risk to the puppies' health and well-being).

If you're buying a puppy, ask how the puppies are handled. Each puppy should spend one-on-one time every day with at least one person. He should begin potty training no later than the seventh week; many breeders start much earlier than that. If you want a well-adjusted adult Shetland Sheepdog, do not get one who hasn't been handled between the seventh and twelfth weeks, and don't take one home at this age if you can't spend lots of time with him. (See also "Socialization" in Chapter 6). If you are buying or adopting a Sheltie who is older than 16 weeks, be sure

Before you bring your new Sheltie home, pet-proof your home and yard to ensure his safety.

that he has been introduced to other people, animals, and places during those first four months.

Another factor that may affect when your puppy can come home with you is a developmental stage known as the fear imprint period. During this period, a puppy is easily frightened by new or strange things in his environment. Anything that scares or hurts him during these periods is imprinted on his mind and may remain frightening to him throughout his life, so it's important to minimize negative experiences at these times. Puppies go through several fear periods, the first around the age of eight weeks. Because it is often the most influential of the fear periods and may not be the best time to introduce changes into a puppy's life, many breeders prefer to keep their Sheltie pups until they are well through this critical time.

PREPARING YOUR HOME AND YARD

Your new Sheltie is coming home! But first, you have some work to do. Start by putting breakables and attractive nuisances out of reach. Many plants are toxic, so keep your Sheltie out of gardens and compost, and put houseplants out of reach. Minimize your use of chemicals in your yard, follow directions carefully, and keep your dog away from areas of use according to the manufacturer's information (call their information number or consult your vet if in doubt).

Dogs, especially puppies, swallow all sorts of things that can harm or kill them: medications, vitamins, tobacco products, pins, needles, yarn, razor blades, the list goes on. Store herbicides, pesticides, antifreeze, paint, solvents, and petroleum products securely, and clean spills thoroughly. Keep hazards, including waste, out of reach.

SHOPPING FOR YOUR SHELTIE

Before bringing your puppy or adult Sheltie home, you must prepare for his arrival. Having everything ready in advance will help to ensure that your pet's transition to a new and unfamiliar environment is as comfortable and stress-free as possible.

Crate

A crate (also called a carrier or cage) is the best tool you can use to keep your unsupervised pup and your belongings safe. Used properly, it will speed up potty training, make traveling safer, and give your dog a refuge. Although people may resist the idea of crating because they wouldn't like to be so confined, most dogs like the den-like environment of their crates for reasonable periods of time. (See "Crate Training" in Chapter 6).

Your dog should have room to stand up, lie down, and turn around comfortably in his crate, but he doesn't need much more than that. Be sure the door fits well and latches securely so that it can't be opened and paws and teeth can't get caught. Fabric crates are handy for travel, but not recommended for puppies. Some dogs like bedding in their crates; others don't. Small washable nonslip rugs make great crate bedding.

Food and Bowls

You'll need dog food, of course. Talk to your breeder, rescuer, or vet about appropriate food for your dog. Treats in reasonable amounts are good for training, but too many treats can quickly lead to a chubby Sheltie, so don't overdo them. (See Chapter 4.)

You'll also need bowls for food and water. Plastic bowls cause allergic reactions in some dogs, and some ceramic products made outside the United States contain toxins that can leach into food and water. Stainless steel bowls are easy to clean, resist chewing, and will last the life of your Sheltie and beyond.

Collar and Leash

Your dog needs at least one collar and leash. Nylon collars are inexpensive and come in a kaleidoscope of colors. Check the fit often, especially if your Sheltie is young and growing, and readjust or replace the collar when necessary. Nylon leashes are inexpensive, but some of them can burn or cut the skin. Don't use a chain leash because it will be ineffective for training and can injure your Sheltie (or you). Most experienced trainers use a 4- to 6-foot (1- to 2-m) leather leash, a quarter- to half-inch (0.6- to 1.3-cm) wide for a Sheltie. Always leash your Sheltie when he's not indoors or inside a fenced area. Don't underestimate how quickly he can dash off and be seriously hurt or killed.

Identification

Attach an identification tag with your phone number, as well as your dog's rabies and license tags, to his collar. Your veterinarian can insert a microchip—a transmitter about the size of a grain of rice—under the skin over your dog's shoulder blade to provide permanent identification, or you can have your dog tattooed with an identifying number, normally on the belly or flanks. For more information, talk to your vet or the following organizations:

- PETtrac/AVID Microchips, 800-336-2843, www.avidmicrochip.com
- HomeAgain MicroChips/Companion Animal Recovery, 800-252-7894, www.public.homeagain.com
- Tatoo-A-Pet, 800-828-8667, www.tattoo-a-pet.com
- National Dog Registry, 800-NDR-DOGS, www.natldogregistry.com

Grooming Supplies

To keep your Sheltie looking gorgeous, you'll need a pin brush, a slicker brush, nail clippers and possibly a Dremel tool or file, a mild dog shampoo, and doggy tooth care products. You may also want a flea comb and a tick remover.

Toys

Don't forget the fun stuff—toys and chews. Puppies and some adult dogs love to chew, and well-made chew toys, like Nylabone products, are safe and long-lasting. Replace toys when they develop cracks, sharp points, or edges, or become small enough

Buying a Crate

A crate is one of the most useful items you will ever purchase for your dog. In addition to being an invaluable housetraining tool, a crate provides a safe place for your dog to stay when you are not at home or when you cannot supervise him. In fact, most dogs enjoy the den-like environment of their crates because it makes them feel safe.

When shopping for a crate, be certain that it is well constructed and big enough for your Sheltie to stand, turn around, and lie down comfortably. If you're not sure what size to buy, ask your pup's breeder or other people who have dogs of similar size.

If your dog will travel in your car a lot, you may find that it's more practical to buy two crates—one for the house and one for the car—than to have to move a single crate back and forth all the time. Either plastic or wire will work in a car, although a plastic airline-approved crate will provide better protection for your dog in case of an accident.

Shopping for Your New Dog

No doubt you'll buy lots of other stuff for your Sheltie as time goes by, but to get started you'll need the following supplies:

- at least one crate (possibly one for home and one for the car)
- bedding for inside the crates and out
- a collar with a name tag attached
- at least one leash
- safe toys and chews
- high-quality food and treats
- safe, nonbreakable bowls for food and water

for your dog to swallow. Most Shelties like to play with furry and squeaky toys, but beware of plastic eyes, synthetic stuffing, and squeakers that can injure your dog if he swallows them.

TRAVELING—OR NOT—WITH YOUR SHELTIE

Shelties love to go wherever their people go, and because of their small size they are easy to take along. Here are some tips to make traveling with your Sheltie easier and safer for everyone.

Traveling by Car

Letting your Sheltie ride loose in your vehicle is risky. An unrestrained dog can be thrown if you hit the brakes, hurting himself or someone else. Likewise, allowing a dog to ride on the driver's lap or on the back window shelf is especially dangerous. It's much safer for your Sheltie to ride in a crate, and a Sheltie-size crate will fit easily into any car. A secure crate will not only shield your dog from injuries in case of collision, but will keep him secure afterward. The last thing you want after an accident is for your dog to get loose when someone opens a car door. If you are injured in an accident, having your Sheltie safely crated will make it easy for someone to take him to a safe place. Second best is a properly fitted doggy seatbelt, which will keep your dog from being thrown around or let loose in an accident, although it won't protect him as well as a crate can. If you use a seatbelt, strap your Sheltie into the back seat. Dogs, like small children, can be injured or killed by a deploying air bag.

When you take your Sheltie along in the car, be sure you won't have to leave him there when you park in warm weather. Even with the windows slightly open, the temperature in a parked vehicle can become lethal for your dog in just a few minutes. In warm weather, leave your Sheltie safely at home if he won't be able to get out of the car with you.

Traveling by Air

Flying somewhere that you want to take your dog? If your Sheltie is small, he may be able to travel in the cabin with you in an approved carrier that will fit under the seat, but if he's too big for that he will have to travel as cargo. All dogs traveling by air must travel in an airline-approved carrier with food and water containers. Your dog will need a health certificate issued by a veterinarian within ten days prior to the flight, and most airlines limit the number of animals allowed on any flight, so make your reservations in plenty of time. Whether he rides in the cabin or in cargo, your Sheltie should wear identification, and you should carry a leash with you. Different carriers have different policies and not all airlines transport animals, so check with the airline well in advance for booking requirements, prices, restrictions, and so on.

Travel Etiquette

When you take your Sheltie into the community, remember that your behavior as a dog owner affects the rights of all of us. Many public places no longer allow dogs because their people behaved badly. Most offensive are those who don't clean up after their dogs. Whether in your own neighborhood or during travel, especially during hotel and motel stays, be courteous to others and be mindful of the fact that not everyone loves pets. Don't leave your dog alone to bark or cause problems. Bring a sheet to spread over beds or chairs, or crate your dog, so you don't leave Sheltie hair behind, and properly clean up any messes your dog has made in your room or elsewhere.

Letting your Sheltie ride loose in your vehicle is risky. Secure your dog in a carrier or with a properly fitted doggy seatbelt for his safety as well as yours.

If you are away from home often or can't take your dog with you when you travel, a qualified pet sitter or doggy day care facility may be the answer.

Pet Sitting and Boarding Options

There are times when our dogs simply can't come along, and fortunately some acceptable options are available. A boarding kennel may be a safe alternative to taking your dog along if you choose carefully. Ask for recommendations, and tour the facility ahead of time. Unless you have asked to house more than one dog together, your Sheltie should have a kennel run to himself. Facilities should be clean, and fresh water should always be available. The entire kennel area should be fenced so that if your dog slips out of his run, he'll still be confined. Plans should be in place to handle emergencies and potential disasters and to prevent theft or vandalism. Someone should be on-site at all times. Some kennels charge for extra services, so be sure you understand what the basic fees include and how much the extras will cost. One drawback to boarding kennels is that many still require certain vaccinations that not all owners want their dogs to have. While you naturally want to be sure that dogs in the facility are healthy, if you prefer not to vaccinate your dog every year, or to omit certain vaccinations (see also Chapter 8), then boarding may not be an option for your dog.

A good pet sitter is another option. Some sitters visit a specified number of times each day, take your dog out, feed him, and play with him; others stay in your home. If you need to find a sitter, ask your vet or groomer for recommendations. Have the prospective sitter visit your home to be sure she's comfortable with your Sheltie and vice versa. Discuss what she's willing to do—feed, give medications, take your dog for walks, play, cuddle, groom—and, if she won't be staying in your house, discuss how often she'll visit and whether you can check in with her daily while you're away. Ask about her experience with dogs and as a pet sitter, and check her references. Ask if she's bonded (she should be), and whether she's affiliated with one of the national pet sitters' organizations. Find out whether she's had canine first aid training, and if she's prepared to handle emergency procedures. Your pet sitter should also have access to a reliable vehicle that can accommodate your pet if needed. After getting all of this information, follow your instincts. Your Sheltie will be happier and safer at home only if he gets gentle, reliable care.

THE IMPORTANCE OF PLANNING AHEAD

Taking the time to choose your Sheltie carefully and to plan ahead for his arrival in your home will pay off in many ways. You'll be more confident that you've chosen the right breed and dog, and more comfortable about fitting your new canine companion into your home and lifestyle. Planning and shopping ahead of time will let you spend more time with your pup when you bring him home. Finally, knowing how to help your Sheltie adapt to his new home, and how to keep him safe and comfortable whether you're home or not, will help you both rest easier.

FEEDING
Your Shetland Sheepdog

If genetics create the basic blueprint for the dog your Shetland Sheepdog can become physically, food and exercise provide the materials necessary to build and maintain that potential. From before he's even born through old age, the food he eats and the exercise his body gets affect your Sheltie's health and behavior. Many common problems can be linked to food, including dry skin and coat, itchiness, hot spots, loose stools, hyperactivity, and lack of energy. A healthful diet will go a long way toward keeping your Sheltie healthy and happy.

BASIC CANINE NUTRITION

What's the best diet for your Sheltie? Good question! And the answers you get will depend on whom you ask. In fact, there are many healthful approaches to canine nutrition, and the correct answer ultimately depends on your preferences and your individual dog's needs. The best way to ensure that your Sheltie eats properly is to learn some basic facts about canine nutrition and observe how your dog looks and acts.

Like all dogs, your Shetland Sheepdog is a carnivore, meaning that in the wild dogs eat mostly prey animals. Although many generations of selective breeding by human beings have modified some of his traits, he is basically designed to be a hunter. His long canine teeth ("fangs") are perfect for slashing and holding prey. His molars aren't much good for chewing, but their sharp, serrated edges easily shear off hunks of meat, and his strong jaws are able to crack bone and dismember joints. His digestive system is very efficient at digesting meat proteins, which constitute the bulk of a wild canid's diet. Your Sheltie probably enjoys fruits and veggies, but his digestive system cannot break down the tough cellulose walls of raw vegetable matter. In the wild, carnivores eat all parts of their prey, including the partially digested vegetable matter in their stomachs and intestines, and so they consume a complete diet. For domesticated carnivores like your Sheltie, cellulose must be broken down through cooking so that his digestive system can use those nutrients in vegetables and fruits that are essential for a dog's health. In fact, an all-meat diet would quickly damage your Sheltie's health because he needs a balanced diet of carbohydrates, fats, minerals, proteins, vitamins, and water.

A well-balanced, nutritious diet will help your dog look and feel his best.

Carbohydrates

Carbohydrates provide energy and are found mostly in plant matter, including grains and fruits. Common sources of carbohydrates in commercial dog foods include corn, soy beans, wheat, and rice. Unfortunately, some dogs are allergic to one or more of these common grains (see also "Allergies" in Chapter 8). Commercial foods that offer alternative sources of carbohydrates are also available, and may include potatoes, oats or oatmeal, and various other grains, vegetables, and fruits. A wide variety of carbohydrate sources can, of course, be used in a homemade diet.

Fats

Dietary fats are an important part of your Sheltie's diet. Fats insulate his internal organs against cold and help to cushion them. Fats also provide energy and help to carry vitamins and other nutrients to his organs through the bloodstream. Too much fat in the diet, however, contributes to obesity, and if excess fat replaces proper amounts of protein in the diet, the dog may eventually become malnourished. Meats, milk, butter, and vegetable oils are rich sources of essential dietary fats.

Minerals

Minerals build bones and keep them strong. They also strengthen cell tissue and help organs function properly. On the other hand, any excess of minerals in your dog's diet really is too much of a good thing and can cause serious problems, particularly in growing puppies. If your dog eats a high-quality diet, he's unlikely to suffer a mineral deficiency, and you should never give him vitamin or mineral supplements unless advised to do so by your veterinarian.

Proteins

Proteins, which are critical building blocks for a healthy, lean body, are composed of amino acids found in meat products and, to a lesser extent, in plants. The best sources of complete proteins are meats, fish, poultry, milk, cheese, yogurt, fish meal, and eggs. About 18 to 25 percent of your dog's diet should be protein.

Vitamins

Vitamins are chemical compounds that support good health. High-quality dog foods provide vitamins in the proper amounts, but light, heat, moisture, and rancidity can destroy vitamins, so it's important to store food properly and to use it before its expiration date. Fruits and the livers of most animals are rich in vitamins. As with minerals, feed your Sheltie a high-quality diet and don't give him vitamin supplements unless your veterinarian advises you to do so.

Water

Although we don't always think of water as a nutrient, it is critical for life and good health. Your Sheltie gets much of his water directly by drinking, but he also uses metabolic water, which is the water released from food as it is digested. Except during

Nutritional Supplements

If you feed your Sheltie a high-quality diet, nutritional supplements are probably unnecessary and may be harmful. Too much calcium, for example, can permanently damage growing bones in puppies and may contribute to kidney stones and other problems in adult dogs. Some vitamins, especially A and D, are toxic in large amounts, and vitamin supplements may cause hypervitaminosis (an excess of vitamins). If you think your dog needs a supplement, talk to your vet first.

housetraining (see Chapter 6), your Sheltie should have access to clean, cool water at all times. He loses water throughout the day through panting as well as elimination, and he must take in an equal amount of water to keep his body in balance and his organs functioning properly.

COMMERCIAL DOG FOODS

Pet food is big business. Walk the dog food aisle of any pet supply, grocery, or "big box" store and you'll find a mind-boggling range of options. Watch an evening of television or pick up a magazine and chances are you'll see puppies and dogs who are cute or gorgeous or lively, apparently all because they eat the advertiser's product. On the other hand, sign onto any canine e-mail list and sooner or later there will be a discussion about dog food, and someone will practically accuse you of cruelty if you feed a commercial dog food.

The truth is that commercial dog foods vary widely in nutritional quality. Some use such low-quality ingredients that they're the canine equivalent of junk food. Some use human-grade ingredients and shun fillers, dyes, and other chemicals. Most, including many of the big-name foods, lie somewhere in the middle.

Very inexpensive foods are made of poorer-quality ingredients, fewer meat proteins, more fat, and more fillers. Your Sheltie may seem to thrive on such a food for a while because the high-fat diet provides energy. But over time he will become malnourished from the lack of protein, vitamins, and minerals. As a result, he will probably develop some of the health and behavior problems that malnutrition causes, including cancer, allergies, hyperactivity, lethargy, and damage to various organs. Trying to save money by buying the cheapest dog foods really is penny wise and pound foolish, and in the long run may compromise your dog's health and shorten his life.

Higher-quality dog foods use higher-quality ingredients and contain few if any fillers, chemicals, or dyes. Such foods tend to be more easily digested, so your dog will benefit more from the nutrients they contain. He will also produce smaller, harder stools, making cleanup easier, and he'll be less flatulent, making the time you spend with him more pleasant. Higher-quality foods cost more per bag or can than do lesser-quality foods, but because better foods are more nutritionally dense, your dog won't need to eat as much per meal.

As with any product, although good quality costs more than poor, the most expensive dog foods aren't necessarily the best for your dog. All those heart-grabbing pet food commercials and ads for big-name dog foods cost a lot of money, and the consumer pays the bill. Most pet supply stores carry a number of less well-known foods that offer higher-quality ingredients at a lower cost than some of the highly advertised "premium" foods, so shop around in a pet supply store, read the labels, and make an informed choice.

Dry foods provide the most popular and diverse meal base for dogs.

Dry Food

Commercial dog foods come in four common forms: dry, semi-moist, canned, and frozen.

Dry dog food, known as kibble, is the least expensive of the commercial offerings (when compared to the equivalent quality of canned or frozen foods), and it offers several advantages. Dry food does not need to be refrigerated, although it does need to be stored in an air-tight container, protected from heat and light, and used by its expiration date. It's easy to measure and easy to pack and carry, and most brands are relatively easy to find if you're traveling. Again, assuming you feed a high-quality dry food without fillers, your dog will have firmer, smaller, less smelly stools, making housetraining easier for him and cleanup after he eliminates easier for you.

Semi-Moist Food

Semi-moist dog foods come in soft chunks, usually packaged in serving-size packets. Most of these foods have little to recommend them. For the same price, you can buy a much better quality of dry food. Dogs who eat semi-moist foods have larger, softer, smellier stools than those fed kibble, and they may have a high incidence of gum disease and tooth decay because the soft food tends to stick to the teeth. Many semi-moist foods contain dyes (to make them look good to you—your Sheltie doesn't care what color his food is), and chemical preservatives and fillers that your dog just doesn't need. Kibble, canned, or frozen foods are better for your dog.

Canned Food

Canned dog foods (sometimes called "wet" foods) are the most expensive of the commercial options, mostly because the water they contain and the cans they come in increase their weight and make shipping more costly. Canned foods are useful for dogs with certain medical conditions, and they can be mixed into kibble to make it more attractive to poor eaters. A diet of strictly canned food, however, can contribute to bad breath, tartar buildup and gum disease, flatulence, and large, soft, smelly stools. Open cans must be refrigerated, and empty cans add considerably to the volume of garbage generated by feeding your dog.

Special Formula Commercial Foods

What about all those "special formula" dog foods you see advertised? There seem to be foods out there for every sort of dog: puppies, seniors, small dogs, big dogs, active dogs, fat dogs, and even dogs of specific breeds. What's next: separate foods for different coat colors? For the most part, this mind-boggling array of different foods is a marketing ploy to attract buyers. If you compare labels, many of these "specialized" formulas are nearly, if not completely, identical to other commercial formulas. Even where they differ to some extent, their "special benefits" are often debatable. For instance, there is no scientific evidence that senior formulas improve the health or longevity of aging dogs. Sometimes these "special" foods may even hurt your dog. Very few dogs— even those who always seem to be busy—need the extra calories and protein found in "active" foods, and most knowledgeable breeders and vets prefer to feed puppies a high-quality maintenance food rather than a higher-calorie "puppy formula."

Another category of special foods, however, do benefit certain dogs. These are the prescription diets designed for dogs with specific health problems. Some, such as those designed for dogs with kidney problems, are available only through veterinarians. Others are more widely available, including a number of foods

How to Read Dog Food Labels

To make sense of dog food labels, you need to know the lingo. Here's a guide to the basics.

Alpha tocopherol:	Vitamin E, a natural preservative
Animal fat:	Fat obtained from the tissue of mammals and/or poultry in the commercial process of rendering or extracting
Beef tallow:	Fat from the tissue of cattle
Brewer's rice:	Small bits of rice broken off from larger kernels of milled rice
Brewer's yeast:	Dried, nonfermentive by-product of brewing beer and ale
Brown rice:	Unpolished rice left after kernels have been removed
Chicken:	Flesh and skin (with or without bone) without feathers, heads, feet, or entrails
Chicken by-product meal:	Ground, rendered, clean poultry parts, including necks, feet, undeveloped eggs, and intestines
Chicken fat:	Fat from the tissue of chicken
Chicken meal:	Dry ground clean combination of chicken flesh and skin with or without bones
Dehydrated chicken:	Dried fresh chicken flesh (without skin, bones, feathers, heads, feet, or entrails)
Dried beet pulp:	Residue after sugar is removed from sugar beets (used as filler)
Fish meal:	Dried ground tissue of undecomposed whole fish or fish cuttings, which may or may not have oil removed
Meat:	Flesh of slaughtered animals, including muscle, tongue, diaphragm, heart, esophagus, overlying fat, skin, sinew, nerves, and blood vessels
Meat by-products:	Clean nonmeat parts of slaughtered animals, including lungs, spleen, kidneys, brain, liver, blood, bone, stomach, and intestines (does not include hair, horns, teeth, or hooves)
Poultry by-products:	Nonmeat parts of slaughtered poultry, such as heads, feet, and internal organs (does not include feathers)

designed to eliminate common allergens from the diets of dogs with food sensitivities (see also "Allergies" in Chapter 8). Many of these have no preservatives or fillers and contain oatmeal or barley instead of corn, wheat, or soy, or replace beef, lamb, and chicken with alternative meat proteins such as duck, fish, or venison.

NONCOMMERCIAL DIETS

If you like puttering in the kitchen and are good at planning and organizing, then you may enjoy preparing a homemade diet for your Sheltie. It's important, though, to do your homework to be sure that your dog eats a balanced diet that will keep him healthy. While he doesn't need to eat a completely balanced diet every day, he does need the proper balance of protein, carbohydrates, fats, essential fatty acids, minerals, and vitamins over the course of each week. Proper nutrition is important throughout your dog's life, and it is critical during the first year, when poor nutrition can cause permanent damage to the skeletal system and organs, resulting in lifelong health problems.

A complete discussion of nutritious homemade diets can fill an entire volume, so only a brief introduction to the topic is offered here. A number of books and websites offer accurate information, guidelines, and recipes for homemade diets, but be cautious and read several sources before you begin. Some sources are based more on opinion than science. It's best to consult your veterinarian, or a veterinary nutritionist, before changing your dog's diet.

Home Cookin'

If you want to control the ingredients that go into your Sheltie's diet, if you don't mind shopping for and preparing the food, and if you have room to store the ingredients and prepared foods properly, then home-cooked doggy meals made from fresh ingredients in your own kitchen may appeal to you. Random table scraps do not make a nutritional diet, but a carefully balanced regimen of high-quality meats, eggs, cooked vegetables, fruits,

A carefully designed home-cooked diet can have many advantages for dogs with special needs. Check with your vet to make sure that this type of diet is right for your Sheltie.

dairy products, and possibly grains can provide sound nutrition and prevent some of the problems associated with certain ingredients in low-quality commercial dog foods, such as common allergies.

A number of books and websites offer recipes for home-cooked meals and treats, or you can develop your own recipes based on your study of canine nutrition.

Aging and Changing Dietary Needs

If your senior Sheltie is healthy and in good condition, there's no need to change his diet just because of his age. In fact, there is no scientific evidence that "senior" dog foods benefit most older dogs any more than a high-quality adult maintenance food. However, if your older Sheltie loses weight, shows signs of change in his skin or coat, or shows other signs of insufficient diet, talk to your vet. Some elderly dogs who cannot digest their food properly suffer from malnutrition even when eating a high-quality diet. They often improve when given a more digestible food, or one with higher caloric density. Splitting the older dog's daily ration into three or four meals throughout the day may also help.

Raw Diets

One rather popular type of homemade diet for dogs is the raw diet, which is composed of uncooked meats and unprocessed fruits and vegetables. Typically, a dog on a raw diet eats raw chicken and turkey bones, with additional organ meat (liver, kidney, heart, brain, tongue, and tripe) and eggs from time to time. Other common ingredients include green leafy vegetables, which must be run though a food processor or juicer first, vegetable oils, brewer's yeast, kelp, apple cider vinegar, fresh and dried fruits, and/or raw honey. Some people also add occasional small servings of grain such as rice or oatmeal, and dairy products, especially raw goat milk, cottage cheese, and plain yogurt. Vitamin and mineral supplements may also be added.

A well-balanced raw diet can provide proper nutrition, but also poses some serious challenges. To ensure that the diet is in fact balanced and complete, you must consult reliable sources of information on canine nutrition and, using the information as a guide, build a diet that includes a wide variety of foods and supplements in the proper proportions. You need time to prepare meals—after all, your Sheltie has to eat every day, no matter how busy you are. You need to store ingredients and prepared meals properly to prevent spoilage. You must also be fastidious about cleanup, especially when handling raw meats and poultry, which contain bacteria that can cause food poisoning and, sometimes, contain parasites that can attack both dog and human members of the family. For safety, you must keep all utensils, work spaces, and dog dishes scrupulously clean, and you must wash your hands with soap and hot water after you handle them. You also need to be aware that cooked bones aren't the only ones that can splinter; raw bones, too, especially poultry bones, can produce shards that can injure or kill your Sheltie.

WHEN TO FEED YOUR SHELTIE

If you ask your Shetland Sheepdog when he should eat, he'll probably say "Now!" But you are in charge of his meals, and it's your job to feed him on a schedule that fits into your own while also promoting his health and well-being. Let's look at the options.

Free-Feeding

Establishing a feeding schedule ensures that your dog is maintaining optimum nutrition and weight by allowing you to monitor and control how much he is eating.

Many people think that dogs who have access to food all the time won't overeat. Not true! Sure, some dogs stay slim and trim even when free-fed, but many respond to their genetic programming as opportunistic eaters. In the wild, predators must eat as much as possible when they can because they may go days without making a kill. In such circumstances, even if they gorge themselves when food is available, their average daily caloric intake will not be excessive. But with domestic dogs, perpetual access to food often results in obesity because there's food today, and there's food tomorrow. Ironically, some free-fed dogs become picky eaters because they know the bowl will always be full, and that makes it less interesting.

Free-feeding is also less than practical if you travel

	Puppies	Adolescents	Active Adults	Sedentary Adults	Seniors
Shetland Sheepdog Feeding Chart					
Age	(7 weeks to 4 to 6 months)	(4 to 6 months to 18 months)	(2 to 7+ Years)	(2 to 7+ years)	(7 years and older)
Times per day	3 or 4	2 to 3	2	2	2 to 4
Best food	High-quality adult maintenance diet, or high-quality puppy formula until 4 to 6 months	High-quality adult maintenance diet	High-quality adult maintenance diet	High-quality adult maintenance diet in moderation; low-calorie adult food in some cases	Adult maintenance diet; senior formula if desired

with your dog or board him when you're away. Boarding facilities feed on a schedule, and the change from free to limited access to food just adds more stress to the boarding experience for your dog.

If your Sheltie has any issues with behaviors such as resource guarding or aggression (see Chapter 6), free-feeding can make the problem worse because your dog may forget that you control his food. If you are attempting to housetrain him, lack of a regular meal schedule will make the job more difficult. In addition, not eating is often the first sign that a dog is ill, and it may not be obvious for a while that your free-fed dog has stopped eating. Finally, food left out can spoil, and it often attracts rodents and insects. All in all, the only reason I can see to free-feed is to save time, but if you don't have time to feed your dog every day, you really don't have time for a dog.

Scheduled Feeding

Feeding your Sheltie on a regular schedule will give you better control over his food intake and therefore his weight. It will make you better able to monitor your dog's health because you'll know immediately if he stops eating, and you'll also be able to monitor how much he's eating. Scheduled meals make housetraining easier to achieve and maintain because regular meals result in regular elimination. If you use food treats to reward and motivate your dog when training, he will find them more inviting if he can't grab a snack whenever he pleases. Finally, reinforcing your status as the benevolent giver of all things at meal and treat times will strengthen your relationship with your dog and make him feel more secure.

On the other hand, clean, fresh water, in contrast to food, should always be available to your dog except in special situations. While you are housetraining a puppy or an adopted adult, you should limit water intake before bedtime to reduce the number of nighttime outings (or accidents). If your Sheltie will be undergoing certain veterinary procedures, especially those requiring anesthesia, your vet will have you withhold water for a certain period. Otherwise, water is essential for your dog's health and should always be available.

Scheduling Mealtimes

There is no single "correct" way to schedule mealtimes for your Sheltie. The number of meals and times you feed them will depend in part on your schedule and in part on your Sheltie's age. Here are some general guidelines to help you structure your dog's mealtimes during different stages in his life.

Feeding Puppies

Young puppies simply can't put enough food into their tiny tummies to supply all the nutrients they need every day to promote healthy growth and development. As a result, they need to eat more frequently than older puppies and adults. Most breeders and vets recommend that puppies 7 to 16 weeks old be given three or four meals spaced evenly throughout the waking hours of the day, with the last meal at least two hours before bedtime to facilitate housetraining. Between four and six months of age, you can cut back to two or three meals a day, and by six months your puppy should do fine on two meals a day. While he is growing and maturing during his first two years, monitor your pup's growth, weight, and condition closely. He should be neither skinny nor fat, and he should have good bone and muscle development. His coat should be shiny, and he should be active and alert.

What You Should Know About Bloat

Bloat (gastric dilatation-volvulus or gastric torsion) is a life-threatening condition that can affect any dog at any age. A bloating dog suffers terrible pain, and without immediate treatment he will go into shock and die. Bloat occurs when a large amount of gas in the stomach creates pressure that causes the stomach to twist, a condition called volvulus or torsion. When torsion occurs, the esophagus is twisted shut and the dog can no longer vomit or belch to relieve the pressure. As pressure continues to build, the flow of blood to and from the heart decreases and the heartbeat becomes erratic. The stomach lining may begin to die, and toxins build up. Disruption in the flow of blood may damage the dog's liver, pancreas, spleen, and bowel, and the stomach may rupture.

Symptoms of bloat or impending bloat include abdominal swelling, retching, salivation, restlessness, refusal to lie down, depression, loss of appetite, lethargy, weakness, and/or rapid heart rate. If you think that your Sheltie may be suffering from bloat, get him to a veterinarian immediately. Call ahead to let them known that you are bringing in a dog you believe to be bloating so that they can be ready to deal with him as soon as you arrive.

Even with veterinary treatment, many dogs who bloat do not recover. Prevention is by far the best cure. Dogs who eat just once a day have an increased risk of bloating, so divide your Sheltie's daily allotment into two or three meals a day. In addition, avoid exercising your dog within two hours of a meal.

Feeding Adolescents and Adults

As your Sheltie matures, he'll need fewer calories per day, even if he is quite active. Interestingly, most pet owners overestimate how active their dogs are. Shelties do tend to be active dogs and sometimes seem to always be in motion. But unless your dog is working sheep for hours every day or hiking the Appalachian Trail with you, you need to keep his food intake, and thus his weight, under control. Adult Shelties should eat two or three times a day. Although some people feed only once a day, dogs who eat that infrequently are at much higher risk than others of bloat.

Feeding Seniors

Although individual dogs age differently, they are usually considered to be seniors at about seven years of age. If your senior Sheltie is healthy and in good condition, there's no reason to change his diet. However, if he is losing weight or having other problems that appear to be food-related, talk to your vet. Weight loss can be a sign that something is wrong physically, especially if it is sudden and unexplained. Some elderly dogs have trouble digesting their food efficiently and can suffer from malnutrition even when eating a high-quality diet. If your vet finds no other medical problem, your dog may benefit from a food with higher caloric density.

Your dog's nutritional requirements are determined by age; puppies will have different needs than adults or seniors.

Older dogs sometimes find food less appealing as their senses, especially their sense of smell, becomes less sharp. If your older Sheltie is healthy but not too keen about eating, try warming his food to make it more fragrant. Pouring a little warm water or unsalted broth over dry kibble or putting food in a microwave for a few seconds works well to soften foods. (Just don't serve the food too hot!) You might also try adding a spoonful of cottage cheese, plain yogurt, or high-quality canned dog food to dry kibble, but watch the calories. Your senior is probably less active than he once was, and you don't want him to gain weight. Some elderly dogs also benefit from smaller, more frequent meals, and I have had several older dogs who didn't care about early breakfasts but snarfed up "brunch" and later meals.

Seniors, especially those with chronic health problems such as arthritis, may suffer from dehydration because getting to the water bowl takes too much effort or is painful. Be sure that your senior Sheltie has easy access to water. Put extra bowls in the places he frequents, and, if necessary, add water to his food.

Whatever his age, if your Sheltie stops eating for more than a day (less if he has a chronic health problem or other obvious signs of illness), consult your vet. Lack of appetite or an unexplained weight change can indicate a serious problem.

SLIM AND TRIM, OR ROLY POLY?

Although your Sheltie may be happy to eat whatever is put before him, there's nothing happy about obesity. Excess weight will not only make your Sheltie look like a furry little tub, but it has also been linked to heart disease, diabetes, pancreatitis, respiratory problems, orthopedic problems, and arthritis. Carrying too many extra pounds around will cause him to overheat more easily and tire more quickly, limiting his ability to enjoy life as he should, and he is likely to die younger than he would if you kept him at a proper weight.

How to Check Your Sheltie's Weight

Extra weight can sneak onto your Sheltie before you realize it, and the early pounds can be easy to miss with that beautiful coat to camouflage them. Even your vet may miss the early signs of excess weight for the same reason. So it's up to you learn to determine whether your dog's weight is appropriate, and to ask your vet if you are unsure.

You can, of course, weigh your Sheltie periodically to see if he's gaining or losing weight. Unfortunately, that won't tell you whether he's too fat, too thin, or just right, so you'll need to

Feed Treats Wisely

Treats in moderation are great; they make your Sheltie happy and that makes you happy. But too many treats will turn your Sheltie into a blimp or a beggar, or both. To keep treats and your dog's weight under control, follow these guidelines:

- Food does not equal love. You can also show affection for your Sheltie with a belly rub, ear scratch, game of fetch, or walk in the park.

- Use treats to reward your Sheltie for doing something more than breathing and looking beautiful. If you want to give him a treat "just because," have him perform an obedience command or cute trick first.

- Treats affect the nutritional balance and total calories of your Sheltie's diet. Limit the number of high-calorie treats you offer, and try low-cal goodies like bits of fresh veggies (carrots and raw green beans work well).

- If your Sheltie has a food allergy, be sure that any treats you give him are free of the allergens. (See also "Allergies" in Chapter 8.)

Beggars Can Be Learners

Most dogs are born with a begging gene, and most people who like dogs are easy targets. Fortunately, dogs are also born with an implicit understanding that life doesn't always give them what they want. It's your job to teach your dog two important lessons that work together. First, he needs to learn that staring and begging won't get you to hand over your food. You can teach this by never rewarding him for begging. If begging never works, he'll stop doing it. This is a case in which "never" really does mean *never*—an occasional bit of food when your dog is being a pest will make him even more persistent next time. This rule applies whether you're snacking on the sofa or eating dinner at the table. If you want to share a little tidbit with your buddy once in a while, that's okay. (Just don't fatten him up on treats!) Wait until you've finished eating, then take your dog to another area, have him do something, like an obedience command or a trick, and then give him a teensy taste. In fact, food can be used as a highly motivating reward. Your Sheltie can't work for money, but he can learn to "work" for food, and he'll be a better, happier companion for it.

use your hands to find out. Begin by placing your thumb on one side of your Sheltie's spine and your index finger on the other just behind his shoulders and then slowly move your fingers along his spine toward his tail. With only enough downward pressure to get through the fur, you should be able to feel the ribs attached to the vertebrae. Next, smooth his coat down along his sides and look down on his back while he's standing (this is especially easy when he's wet, such as after a bath). You should see a distinct "waist" where his body narrows between his ribs and his hips. If you can't feel ribs or see a waist, your Shetland Sheepdog is too fat.

How to Take Off Excess Weight

If your Sheltie puts on some unwanted pounds, don't panic. It is possible to take them off again, and even just a few pounds can make a big difference on a dog the size of a Sheltie. Here are some tips for doggy dieters:

- The guidelines on most packages of commercial dog food recommend more food than the average dog needs. Use them only as rough starting points. If your dog is fat, he needs less food, no matter what the bag says.
- Use a standard measuring utensil to portion your dog's food to be sure he's getting what you think he's getting. If you typically feed him a half a cup (227 g) of kibble per meal, buy an inexpensive set of measuring cups and use the appropriate one to dish up his dinner. If you use a larger cup or scoop and guestimate the measurement, chances are good that you're

feeding your dog more than you think you are.

- To reduce your dog's weight, you must reduce his caloric intake. Most dogs claim to be starving even when they get plenty of food, and, as we've seen, most will overeat whenever possible. It's up to you to see that your Shetland Sheepdog doesn't sacrifice his long-term health to his ancestral appetite.

- If your Sheltie has eaten his allotment of calories, and you really think he's still hungry, there are ways to add bulk without calories to make him feel fuller. You can measure a meal's worth of kibble, divide it in two, and soak one half in water for a half hour or so, letting it absorb water and expand. Then mix the dry portion into the soaked portion and serve. The swollen kibble will take up more room in your dog's stomach, making him feel fuller. Or, mix high-fiber, low-calorie food into your dog's regular food. Good choices that most dogs enjoy include unsalted green beans (uncooked fresh beans or frozen beans are fine; if you use canned beans, rinse them well to remove salt); lettuce or spinach; canned pumpkin (not pie filling, just plain pumpkin); or unsalted, air-popped popcorn (unless your Sheltie is allergic to corn).

- Low-calorie "diet" dog foods are a possibility but are not usually necessary and often are ineffective. Lots of fat dogs stay fat on long-term diets of "light" food because they are fed too

Instead of offering food treats, which add calories, show affection for your dog by offering a special toy, game of fetch, or belly rub.

much of it, along with other treats and snacks that add to the day's intake, and they are not exercised enough. Your Sheltie will probably do better eating smaller quantities of maintenance food and getting more exercise.

• Treats add calories, so limit the number that you feed your Sheltie, and be sure that other members of your household don't give him extras. If you are using treats for training, set aside part of your dog's daily food allowance to use as rewards; most dogs think that a single piece of plain old dog food is special. Another alternative is to use low-calorie treats, such as small bits of raw carrot or green beans, or sugar-free oat cereal.

Age, exercise, general health, and other factors all affect your dog's dietary needs, so it's important to modify his food intake as his nutritional needs change.

Exercise for Weight Maintenance

Most people attribute excess weight to overeating or poor food choices, but lack of sufficient exercise is probably one of the biggest reasons for obesity in pet dogs—and often one of the most overlooked. Good nutrition, along with regular daily exercise, is critical if your Sheltie is to live a healthy life. It will help keep your dog at a proper weight, tone his muscles, build strong bones and maintain his joints, and help keep his cardiovascular and immune systems healthy. While monitoring and adjusting your dog's food intake as needed to keep him at an appropriate weight for his age and activity level is important, so is making sure to schedule daily

Healthy feeding practices combined with daily exercise can keep your dog from becoming overweight.

Should Your Kids Feed the Dog?

A responsible adult should always supervise the feeding of your dog, but in most cases your kids can help. Here are some things you can do to make sure things go smoothly:

- Dogs sometimes think they outrank children, and food can trigger dominance behavior. Teach your child not to feed your dog, including treats, unless a responsible adult is present. If necessary, put dog food and treats out of reach. An adult should always be in a position to intervene immediately whenever a child feeds your dog.
- Teach your child never to tease dogs, especially with food.
- Train your Sheltie to sit and wait politely until your child puts the food down.
- Teach your child to offer dog treats from an open palm.
- Teach your children never to take food (or other things) away from your dog.
- Be sure that an adult supervises the frequency of your dog's meals and their size. Children may overfeed or forget to feed your dog.

Don't put your dog's care entirely in the hands of a child. While pets may help children learn to be responsible, too much pressure about dog-care duties can make a child resentful and unreliable. Ultimate responsibility lies with adults. Your dog should not go hungry, unexercised, or unbrushed if your child forgets, and children lack the judgment and experience to respond to many signs of illness or other problems.

exercise sessions with him, whether it's a walk, game of fetch, or training for a sporting activity.

And, as with all health-related issues, prevention is always preferable to treatment after the fact, so check your dog's weight on a regular basis. If you think that your Sheltie has a weight problem, it is important to take steps to correct it right away. If you think he has a more serious weight issue, discuss an appropriate diet and exercise program with your veterinarian.

LESS IS MORE

Your Sheltie doesn't need fancy cuisine or a high-tech gym setup to stay in optimum physical and mental health, but he does need high-quality nutrients and regular exercise in the right amounts. You can ensure that your dog's diet and exercise routine are right for him by learning about canine nutrition, keeping your dog active, and learning how to evaluate his weight and physical condition. You'll be rewarded with a healthier, happier, longer-lived Shetland Sheepdog.

GROOMING
Your Shetland Sheepdog

One of the things that attracts people to the Shetland Sheepdog is his glorious coat. But keeping the Sheltie's coat—and the rest of him—in good shape does require some effort. The following basic guidelines are meant to help make the grooming process a little easier for both you and your dog.

BENEFITS OF GOOD GROOMING

Proper grooming offers benefits beyond the purely cosmetic. For one thing, grooming sessions are a time for you and your dog to build and reinforce the bond between you. If you're gentle, your Sheltie will learn to love the feel of your touch on his body, just as you love the feel of his fur against your skin. He'll also learn to trust your hands, which is vital in training and in an emergency. Most dogs and people find grooming sessions to be relaxing if the dog has been taught to accept and enjoy the process.

Grooming benefits your Sheltie's health, too. Not only do regular grooming sessions keep him cleaner, but they give you a chance to check him frequently for cuts, bites, bumps, sore spots, fleas and ticks, and other early signs of health problems before they become serious. Regular brushing also minimizes the housework that's part of living with a dog, removing loose hair that would otherwise end up on your furniture, floors, carpets, and clothes.

GROOMING SUPPLIES

As with any job, the right tools make grooming easier and more effective. Here are the basic supplies you will need to keep your Sheltie properly groomed.

Brushes

All sorts of brushes are available to handle different kinds of canine coats. During the spring and fall, when your Sheltie sheds more, you can remove loose hair more quickly with an undercoat rake (a device with short teeth that are aligned along a straight bar attached to a handle). Otherwise, a pin brush (a flat brush with moderately thin pins) does a nice job on the body, and a slicker (also a flat brush, but with shorter, thinner metal pins) works

In addition to keeping your dog clean and healthy, a grooming session offers you a great opportunity to bond with him.

well on the shorter fur of the legs and feet. A coarse metal comb is good for a final touch up. You may want a mat splitter for removing mats, although if you groom your Sheltie regularly you shouldn't need one.

Scissors/Thinning Shears

If you want to do your own trimming, you'll need scissors and possibly thinning shears. Don't buy the cheapest shears—the blades often don't hold a sharp edge and don't meet properly, so they don't cut smoothly. Pet supply and beauty supply stores usually carry reasonably priced shears that, with proper care, will work well for years.

Nail Clippers

Nail care is essential to your Sheltie's health, so you will need good-quality nail clippers. Guillotine clippers have a blade that slides through a small window into which you have inserted your dog's nail. Scissors-style clippers have opposing blades that slide past one another like scissors blades when you squeeze the handles. Both work well, so whichever you choose is a matter of personal preference. You may also want a file to smooth rough edges after trimming—the emery boards sold for use on acrylic nails work well on dog nails.

Dental Care Tools

Dental care tools are an important part of any essential grooming kit. Ask your vet to recommend toothbrushes, plaque removers, and toothpastes that are safe and effective for dogs. (Don't use toothpaste made for people on your Shetland Sheepdog. If he swallows it, he'll get an upset stomach.) If you find a toothbrush difficult to manage, try a dental sponge, which is a small disposable sponge with a flexible handle, or experiment with a "finger brush" that fits over your index finger.

Shampoo and Conditioner

Shampoo formulated for people will dry and damage your Sheltie's skin and coat, so use shampoo formulated for dogs.

Special shampoos are available for certain skin conditions, but unless your vet recommends one, all you need is a good-quality, mild dog shampoo. And here's a little trick: You can save money and make lathering and rinsing easier if you dilute your dog's shampoo before you apply it rather than after. Mix one part shampoo with one or two parts water in a clean squirt bottle, shake well, and apply a small amount of the mixture to your dog's coat. It doesn't take much to get him nice and clean.

You may want a conditioning and detangling product to use after baths and when brushing between baths. Several good products are available that do not need to be rinsed out. Ask your breeder or groomer to recommend one or two.

Ear Cleanser

If your Sheltie seems to produce a lot of ear wax, keep a mild ear cleanser on hand. Ask your vet for recommendations.

Towels/Dryers

You'll need towels to partially dry your dog after baths. Regular bath towels work fine, or you can purchase one or two super-absorbent cloths sold through pet supply stores and other outlets. If you bathe your dog very often, you may want to purchase a high-velocity dryer designed to dry canine fur without burning the skin or hair. You can also use a regular hand-held hair dryer, but always set it on a cool setting so you don't overheat your dog.

Now that you have all the tools, let's look at how they're used.

COAT CARE

Brushing is the basis of good coat care. You may also want to trim the straggly hairs from your Sheltie's coat to keep him looking tidy, and occasionally you may need to deal with a mat or other mess.

Brushing

A thorough brushing two or three times a week during most of the year will help keep your Shetland Sheepdog looking and feeling good. During the spring and fall, when he "blows coat," or molts, daily brushing is essential.

When working with a Sheltie coat, how you brush is as important as how often. Brushing just the long outer guard hairs

Read Product Warnings

The ingredients in some grooming and parasite-prevention products can be hazardous to a puppy or a dog with health problems. Read all instructions and warning labels carefully before using any grooming or flea-prevention products. If in doubt, ask your vet.

leaves the short, dense undercoat prone to matting, and mats are big trouble (see also "Dealing with Burrs, Tangles, and Matts"). Although a small mat or two can usually be removed, a heavily matted coat may have to be completely shaved off.

How to Brush

Begin your brushing session by lightly spritzing your dog's coat with water or a dilute conditioner (a tablespoon of conditioner in 16 ounces [240 ml] of water works well). Dry hair is prone to breakage, and a light misting will also reduce static in the coat, making it easier to work with.

Starting at the front of your dog, use a pin brush to part a narrow strip of hair down to the skin. Gently brush the hair toward your dog's head, drawing the pins from the roots to the tips. Your dog may be more comfortable lying on one side while you work on the other, or you can brush while he's standing. Work your way from front to rear in narrow strips. Then, starting near your dog's rear end, brush the hair back into its normal position, working your way forward in sections. You can work your way through his long chest hair in much the same way, starting at the throat and brushing narrow strips upward and then smoothing the hair back into position.

The long feathers on your Sheltie's tail and the backs of his legs also need attention. Work in small sections and brush from the bone to the tips of the hair. When you've worked through all the sections, smooth the hair together with the brush.

You can use a fine-toothed comb on the short hair of your dog's head to remove dead hair, and a slicker brushed against the direction of growth will work well on the fronts of his legs. Don't push so hard that you scratch his skin.

Dealing With Burrs, Tangles, and Mats

Burrs and other types of plant matter caught in your Sheltie's lovely coat can be very hard to remove, especially if they've been there for some time. Some burrs are so sharp and tough that they will cut into your dog's skin (and your fingers) before they'll let go. If only a few are present, and they aren't too tightly wound up in hair, try to tease the hair away from them a little at a time with your fingers and a metal comb or slicker brush. Some burrs get so tightly caught that they have to be cut out. The safest way to do this

---

Combine Grooming With a Health Check

In addition to making your dog look and feel good, grooming time also offers an opportunity to do a regular health check. Taking a few minutes to examine your dog before you groom him can alert you to physical changes that may indicate a problem.

So, before you begin grooming your Sheltie, run your hands over his body and check for any sensitive areas, lumps, bumps, or unusual dry patches or bald spots. Check his teeth and gums to see if they are in good condition, and look for broken or overgrown teeth or signs of redness or swelling in his gums. Check his eyes, ears, and nose for unusual discharge. If you find something questionable, contact your vet right away—it's much better to treat minor problems before they become serious health issues.

is to use blunt-tipped scissors, such as baby nail scissors. If you use pointed scissors, aim the sharp tips away from your dog's face and body, as well as your own. Be careful, too, not to cut into the skin with the edges of the blades. To protect your dog's skin, try to slide a comb under the burr first, so that the comb's teeth are between the scissors and the skin.

Mats, too, sometimes sneak into even the best-kept fur coat, and if you miss a week or two of grooming, you're almost sure to find one or two. Not only do mats pull and make your dog look unkempt and feel uncomfortable, they can trap moisture against the skin, creating an ideal environment for bacteria, fungi, and some parasites. Eventually, hot spots, open sores, and infections can set in. To remove a mat, begin by spraying it with detangler or leave-in conditioner. Then, lift the mat with your fingers and work the teeth of a slicker brush into it, wriggling the slicker from side to side. Remove it, then reinsert it. Do this several times to loosen the mat, then see if you can brush or comb the hairs free, starting at the edges and working inward. If you're patient, and the mats aren't too big or too plentiful, you can probably work them out this way. If not, you will need to cut them out using the method described earlier for removing burrs.

A thorough brushing two or three times a week will help keep your Sheltie looking and feeling good.

If you do have to resort to cutting burrs or mats from your dog's fur, be very careful—it's all too easy to catch skin in scissors blades. If you aren't sure you can do the job safely, take your dog to a professional groomer.

Trimming

A few strategic snips to tidy straggly hairs will give your Sheltie a more polished look, keep his feet cleaner and healthier, give him better traction on slippery surfaces, and reduce the amount of dirt and debris he brings into the house.

To trim the front feet, use a slicker to brush gently against the

direction of growth and to pull the hair up and away from your dog's toes. The long hairs between the toes will stand up when you do this. Then, use your thinning shears to trim the long hairs so that they are about one-half to three-quarters of an inch long (1.3 to 1.9 cm) and level with the top of the foot. Next, use your thinning shears to trim any long hairs from the edges of the foot. Finally, lift each foot and, using regular hair-cutting scissors, trim the hair around and between the pads. Be careful not to catch the edge of the pad.

The front pastern, which is the portion of leg between the foot and the bottom of the long bones, may also be tidied up by trimming all the hair to one length around the back of the bone. Some people use thinners for this; others prefer straight blades. To trim the hocks, which are the long bones above the feet in the back legs, brush the hair straight back with your slicker and then trim the back so that the edge of the hair parallels the bone.

If your Sheltie has long, straggly hairs on his ears, trim them carefully with your thinning shears, being careful not to pull or cut into the ear itself.

Bath Time

Many people and dogs approach doggy bath time reluctantly, but it doesn't have to be a test of wills and reflexes if you take the time

Doggy Bath Supplies

Gather everything you'll need for your Sheltie's bath before you begin. Here's what you need:

- mild dog shampoo
- cream rinse or detangler
- cotton balls to protect the ear canals
- ophthalmic ointment to protect the eyes from shampoo
- nonslip mat for safety in the tub
- a hose or unbreakable container for rinsing
- one or two towels
- hair catcher for the drain
- a high-speed dryer designed for dogs, or a hand-held hair dryer with a cool setting

to teach your dog that the tub or sink is a safe and not-so-unpleasant place.

Bath Training

Begin bath training as soon as you get your Sheltie, and (hopefully) before you need to bathe him. Put your pup on a nonslip mat in the tub or sink, give him a treat, praise him, and pet him gently. If he struggles to get out, hold him firmly but gently and talk to him quietly. When he stops struggling, give him a treat, tell him he's a good dog, and take him out of the tub. Don't make a fuss or reward him; he's learning to like being in the tub, not out of it. Repeat this process every day for a while, slowly increasing the time he has to stay in the tub. When he's comfortable in the dry tub, add a little lukewarm water so he gets his feet wet, and continue to reward him. When he accepts the "wet feet routine," wet his body with lukewarm water from a sprayer or by pouring water onto him from an unbreakable container, and, again, reward him for accepting it. Like all training, tub training takes time and planning up front, but you'll end up with a dog who isn't afraid, which will make baths easier for both of you.

Before bringing your dog to his bath, have all your supplies set up and ready to go.

How to Bathe Your Sheltie

When you're ready to give a real bath, gather all your supplies before you begin—after all, you can't leave your soapy dog in the tub while you run downstairs for towels!

Before you wet your Sheltie, brush him thoroughly to remove loose hair. If he has any tangles or mats, remove them while they're dry. Gently place a cotton ball into the opening of each ear to protect the ear canal. You can protect his eyes with an ophthalmic ointment (available from your vet, groomer, or pet supply store), or be very careful not to get soap into his eyes. If you do so accidently, rinse his eyes thoroughly with clean water and watch for signs of inflammation or injury for a day or two.

Put your Sheltie into the tub or sink, rewarding him as you did in training. Wet him with lukewarm (not hot) water, then apply dog shampoo and work it in gently with your fingers, beginning at your dog's neck and working toward the tail. Don't scrub in circles or back and forth because you'll end up with a tangled mess. Repeat this with his chest and belly, up under the hind legs, and under his tail. Don't lather his face; instead, use a washcloth to clean it gently and then to remove shampoo.

If you're trying to kill fleas, you don't need to expose your dog to toxic insecticidal shampoo. Instead, wet him and lather him thoroughly with your regular dog shampoo, beginning with a "collar" of lather high on his neck to keep any fleas from leaving his body to hide in his ears. Leave the lather on for about ten minutes to drown the fleas, then rinse.

Rinsing is arguably the most important part of your Sheltie's bath. Shampoo residue can irritate his skin and leave his fur sticky, so run your hands over all parts of your dog after rinsing to be sure you got all the soap out (if it's there, it will feel slick and leave bubbles on your hand). Pay particular attention to those spots where soap loves to hide: armpits, groin, and the groove along the belly between the ribs. When the shampoo is out, gently squeeze the excess water from your dog's coat. Then gently pat out as much moisture as possible with a towel or two.

Shampoo residue can irritate your dog's skin, so rinse his fur thoroughly.

Praise and reward your dog for being so good before you release him, then carefully let him go so that he doesn't hurt himself or something else with a wild leap. It's usually smart to put on a collar and leash before letting go—"crazy

No More Doggy Odor or Doggy Breath

Your Shetland Sheepdog should not smell bad or have bad breath. Unpleasant odors are usually caused by one or more of the following:

- Oil, bacteria, or yeast on the skin: If a bath doesn't help, don't just mask the odor with perfumes. Talk to your vet; your dog may need a special shampoo or medication.

- Ear infections: Have your vet diagnose the infection and prescribe effective treatment.

- Impacted or infected anal glands: Your groomer can express the glands, but if the problem persists, see your vet.

- Gum disease or tooth decay: Regular dental exams and occasional professional cleanings, supported by good home dental care, will prevent most problems and keep your Sheltie's kisses sweet.

- Intestinal or stomach gas: Chronic flatulence is not normal and indicates that your dog is either eating something that doesn't agree with him, or that he has a health problem. A change of food may help (see also Chapter 4); if not, see your vet.

- A foreign substance on the coat and/or skin: If your Sheltie rolls in something foul (a very doggy thing to do!), you'll know he needs a bath. A good doggy shampoo will work on most things, but if he gets into a greasy or oily substance, you may need to use a stronger cleanser. Many wildlife rescuers use Dawn dishwashing liquid to clean up animals caught in oil spills and the like. Don't make it your regular dog shampoo, but it won't hurt for an unexpected heavy-duty cleanup.

dog antics" are common after baths, and most dogs like to run and roll and rub themselves on things (think carpets, walls, furniture, bedspreads, etc.). If your Sheltie needs to go out, take him on leash because wet dogs love nothing better than to roll in the dirt, too.

Drying

Getting your Sheltie dry may take a while. You can, of course, confine him to his crate or a waterproof room away from chilling cold or drafts and let him air dry if you like, but that can take hours. In cool weather, pinning a dry towel around his body will speed up the drying time, but in hot weather that's not a good idea because it holds in too much body heat. You can blow dry the coat if you like, preferably with a high-velocity dryer made for dogs, or a hair dryer on a cool setting.

DENTAL CARE

Gum disease is very common in adult dogs and can contribute to heart, liver, and kidney disease, cause "dog breath," and lead to tooth loss. It develops when bacteria and food particles collect along the gum line and form plaque, which

soon turns to tartar (calculus) and irritates the gums, leading to gingivitis (inflammation of the gum). If tartar builds up under the gums, it causes periodontal disease, resulting in abscesses, infection, and loss of teeth and bone.

Ideally, you should brush your dog's teeth every day to remove the plaque, but doing so even every few days will go a long way toward preventing tartar from forming. Many dental-friendly chews, such as the ones made by Nylabone, also work to reduce plaque and tartar buildup. In addition, make dental checkups part of your Sheltie's routine veterinary care. Your vet will check your dog's teeth and mouth, and he may also recommend thorough cleaning and polishing under anesthesia.

If you have a puppy, check his mouth and teeth every few days. Puppies, like human babies, are born toothless. Their deciduous, or baby, teeth begin to come in at about four weeks, and they are replaced by permanent teeth when the puppy is between three and five months old (see also "Chewing" in Chapter 6). Sometimes a baby tooth isn't pushed out properly by the permanent tooth, and if not removed it will cause the permanent teeth to be misaligned, keep the jaw bones from developing properly, and cause your puppy pain. If you suspect that your Shetland Sheepdog pup has retained a baby tooth, take him to your vet.

How to Brush Your Sheltie's Teeth

Home dental care should be a regular part of your grooming routine, and brushing your dog's teeth isn't as hard as you may think. To begin, put a small amount of doggy toothpaste on your finger and gently rub it along your dog's teeth and gums. Don't use toothpaste made for people because it can cause your dog stomach distress if it's swallowed—and dogs don't spit! The toothpaste tastes good (or so my dogs tell me!), and many dogs look forward to having their teeth cleaned. When your dog seems comfortable with that procedure, switch to a canine toothbrush, which is a bit different from a toothbrush designed for human teeth. As an alternative, you can try a finger brush (a plastic device that fits onto your finger) or even a piece of surgical gauze wrapped around your finger. Gently brush or rub your dog's teeth and gums to clean them much as you would your own. The brushing action begins the cleaning process, and enzymes in the doggy toothpaste continue cleaning after you finish. Start slowly, and always make the process pleasant for your dog. If you're unsure, or you have trouble brushing your dog's teeth, ask your vet to show you the proper technique.

EAR CARE
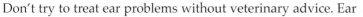

The Shetland Sheepdog's upright ears allow for air circulation, which helps reduce the incidence of ear infections, but some Shelties still occasionally have ear problems. Allergies, hormonal problems, and excess moisture can all promote abnormal growth of yeast or bacteria in the moist, warm ear canal. Ear mites are not common in dogs, but if your Sheltie is sensitive to mite saliva, the bite of even one of these tiny arthropods may make him scratch himself crazy. Active, playful dogs sometimes get dirt, plant matter, or other things in their ears, too, and that can be trouble.

Check your Sheltie's ears at least once a week. The skin lining the inside of the ear should be pink or flesh colored, not red or inflamed. A little wax is normal, but copious wax, dirty looking discharge, or strong or nasty odors are not. If your dog persistently scratches or rubs his head or ears, shakes or tilts his head, or cries or pulls away when you touch his ears or the area around them, he may have an infection or other problem.

Don't try to treat ear problems without veterinary advice. Ear

To keep your Sheltie's ears and eyes healthy and well groomed, make a thorough inspection of them a weekly habit.

infections are painful and can cause permanent hearing loss. To treat an infection effectively, it must be accurately diagnosed. Inappropriate treatment will prolong your dog's discomfort and may also cause more damage, making the infection more difficult to treat later.

How to Care for Your Dog's Ears

If your dog's ears are dirty but not inflamed or sensitive, you can clean them with a mild cleanser designed for canines (ask your vet for a recommendation). Do it outdoors or in a bathroom or other area you can clean easily because ear cleaning can get messy!

Following product directions, squirt ear cleanser into the ear to flush it, then press the ear flap over the opening of the canal and massage for a few seconds to work the cleanser in. Then let go and stand back—most dogs shake their heads, flinging cleaner and wax far and wide. When both ears are cleaned and shaken, gently wipe them with a cotton ball or tissue. *Never* push anything into your dog's ear canals; you could damage the ear drum and cause deafness. If your Sheltie has very waxy ears, or if he plays in water frequently or has a buddy who licks his ears, clean them about once a week. If his ears stay nice and clean on their own, you don't need to do anything except check them regularly.

EYE CARE

Healthy Sheltie eyes are clear and moist, with no sign of redness, swelling, excess tearing, mucous, or squinting, any of which can indicate infection, abrasion, or some other problem. If you notice any of these symptoms, don't wait; take your dog to the vet to prevent permanent damage.

As your Sheltie enters his senior years, his eyes may appear cloudy. This is often due to nuclear sclerosis, a change in the lens associated with aging. It usually does not impair vision. Clouding may indicate a cataract, however, and cataracts can cause partial or complete vision loss. Tell your veterinarian if you see changes in your dog's eyes. Because Shelties are prone to certain inherited eye diseases (see also Chapters 2 and 8), you may want to have your dog's eyes examined periodically by a veterinary ophthalmologist. To save a little money on the exam, ask your local Shetland Sheepdog club, kennel club, or vet about eye clinics in your area.

How to Care for Your Dog's Eyes

You can also do a few things at home to protect your Shetland Sheepdog's eyes and help keep them healthy into old age. First, keep the area around your dog's eyes clean. Mucous deposits at the corners of the eyes can harbor bacteria that may cause eye infection, so gently wipe away "gunk" once or twice a day with a moist washcloth or tissue. Be careful when you bathe your dog or apply any products to his face; soap and other chemicals can cause devastating eye damage. When you travel with your dog, keep him away from open windows. Even a tiny insect or bit of dirt hitting an eye at the speed of a moving vehicle can cause serious, painful injury. For this and other safety reasons, always have your Sheltie travel securely in a crate.

FOOT AND NAIL CARE

Just as a well-brushed Sheltie drops less hair in the house, nicely trimmed nails are less likely to scratch floors or snag carpets or upholstery. Besides, sore feet from overgrown nails are no fun, and trimmed nails can help keep your Sheltie's lovely little paws healthy. Burrs, stones, and other debris can get stuck, especially between the toes and pads, so check your dog's feet frequently, especially after outings. Gently remove foreign matter with your fingers or tweezers. Also, trimming the hair on the bottom of the paws so that it's even with the pads will help keep your dog's feet (and your floors) clean and give him better traction on smooth surfaces.

Keep your Shetland Sheepdog's nails trimmed short. Nails long enough to hit the ground force the toes out of their normal position, distorting the foot and potentially causing lameness and permanent deformity. If you hear the click of nails when your dog walks on a hard surface, it's time for a pedicure.

Nail care keeps your dog's feet healthy. Gradually introduce nail trimming to your Sheltie when he's a puppy so that he can become accustomed to the process.

Nail Care Training

Nail trimming needn't be difficult, and there are some things you can do to keep it that way. First, teach your dog that having his feet handled is no big deal. When you're relaxing together, hold each of your pup's feet one at a time and gently massage and flex his toes. If he objects, hold one foot gently and give him a treat. Be sure you reward him for letting you hold his foot, and not for pulling it away. Do this for a few sessions without trying to trim his nails. When he's comfortable with having his feet held, try trimming one nail. If he doesn't fight you, great! Trim another. But if your dog is still unsure about this, trim just the one nail, give him a treat while you're still holding his foot, then let go. Do another nail later. Be sure to continue paw-holding sessions without trimming, too. Your dog will soon learn that your aren't going to hurt him during this process.

How to Trim Nails

Now for the mechanics of nail trimming. Find a comfortable position and a location where you have sufficient light. Hold your dog's paw gently but firmly, press lightly on the bottom of the foot pad to extend the nail, and trim the very tip, below the quick (which is the living part of the nail). If your dog has light-colored nails, the quick will look pink from the blood vessels inside it. If his nails are dark, cut below the place where the nail narrows and curves downward. Trim the tip, and then look at the end of the nail. If you see a black dot near the center of the nail, you're at the quick and it's time to stop trimming. If not, shave a little more off. Don't forget the dew claws, those funny little toes on the insides of the legs above the front feet.

If you accidentally cut into the quick, stop the bleeding with styptic powder (available from pet supply or drug stores) or corn starch. Put a little in the palm of your hand or a shallow dish and dip the nail into it. The powder will stick to the nail and seal the blood vessel.

Clippers leave sharp, rough edges, but you can smooth them out with a few short, downward strokes of an emery board (the ones made for acrylic nails work well on doggy nails). Some people use a Dremel tool, which is a rotary grinder with interchangeable sandpaper heads to grind and smooth the rough edges off the nail. Although these grinders are not difficult to use, they do get hot,

Anal Sac Care

Ever wonder why dogs sniff each others' fannies? Like other predators, your Sheltie has anal sacs located slightly below his anus. These glands produce a smelly substance whose odor identifies each individual to other dogs. In a healthy dog, the anal glands express, or empty, themselves during every bowel movement, which is why dogs find poop so fascinating—it tells them who else has passed their way.

If the anal sacs don't empty regularly, they become impacted. Impacted glands are not dangerous in themselves, but they are uncomfortable and can cause an affected dog to bite at the area or scoot along the floor, which may injure the delicate tissue surrounding the anus. Impacted anal glands can also make defecation difficult or painful and can lead to a painful infection or abscess.

Impaction can often be relieved by manually expressing the anal sacs by squeezing them gently. The odor of anal gland fluid doesn't appeal to most people as much as it does to dogs, but if you're brave you can have your vet or groomer teach you how to express the glands. You can also have your vet or groomer do the job when necessary.

Chronically impacted anal sacs can sometimes be relieved by a high-fiber diet, which causes bulkier stools that express the glands as they pass. In severe cases, the anal glands can be surgically removed.

and long hair can easily get caught and wrapped tight about the rotating drum, so it's a good idea to have someone with experience show you how to use a Dremel safely and effectively. Keep your nail clippers sharp, and be sure they are properly aligned. Dull or poorly aligned blades won't cut cleanly, and they pinch.

If you're really uncomfortable about trimming your dog's nails, have your groomer or vet do it for you. Just be sure you take your Sheltie in regularly, which is every three to four weeks for most dogs.

HOW TO FIND A PROFESSIONAL GROOMER

There may be times when you'd rather have someone else bathe and trim your Sheltie. Enter the professional groomer. To find a good one you can trust, ask your veterinarian, family, and friends for recommendations. Most groomers are kind and gentle with dogs, but, as in any business, there are unfortunate exceptions, so check the facility and the staff out before you entrust them with your dog. Visit the shop before your appointment if possible. If you don't feel comfortable about a particular groomer or shop, go elsewhere.

When first visiting a groomer, here are things to look for and questions to ask:

- Is the facility clean and reasonably tidy?
- Do they disinfect scissors, nail trimmers, tables, and other equipment between clients?
- Are the animals who are not being groomed housed in safe, secure cages or kennels? Do they have access to fresh drinking water?
- What training and experience do the groomers in the shop have?
- Are the groomers familiar with Shetland Sheepdog grooming?
- What kind of shampoos, conditioners, and other products do they use?
- Do they use a hand-held drier or a cage drier? If a cage drier is used, is someone always present while the dog is exposed to the drier?

If you would rather not groom your dog yourself, seek the services of a professional groomer.

Grooming the Show Sheltie

The grooming tips in this book are meant for Shelties who are not showing in the conformation ring. To learn about caring for and grooming the show dog's coat, consult your breeder. Sheltie clubs often host grooming workshops as well. To find one in your area, go to the American Shetland Sheepdog Association website at www.assa.org/clubs.

- Do they clean the ears?
- Do they check and, if necessary, express the anal glands?
- Do they work without sedatives? (Be very cautious about allowing anyone other than a veterinarian give your Sheltie a sedative!)
- Are they trained in canine first aid? What will they do if something goes wrong?
- How long will your dog need to be there? Where will he be kept when he's not being groomed? Where will he be taken to potty? Is the area clean and fenced?
- What are the fees for a Shetland Sheepdog, and what services are included? (Cost should not be the only consideration, but you don't want any nasty surprises when you pick up your dog.)

The benefits of good grooming more than compensate for the time and effort required. Your house will stay cleaner, and your Sheltie will be healthier and happier. Best of all, he'll look his beautiful best, and that can't help but make you smile.

TRAINING AND BEHAVIOR
of Your Shetland Sheepdog

Nobody wants to live with a brat, even if he's cute, furry, and otherwise devoted. Positive training is the key to keeping your Sheltie from behaving inappropriately, and your training efforts will be more effective if you learn about normal canine behavior and instincts and use that knowledge to teach your dog what you want and don't want from him.

Although it's tempting to ascribe human feelings and motivations to dogs because they live so close to us, the truth is that they have different interests, abilities, and motivations than we do. Almost everything your Sheltie does is either instinctive or learned. (Exceptions would be behaviors that result from outside influences such as illness, injury, or chemicals/drugs.) When we understand this and learn to observe our canine companions as well as they observe us, we'll know how to better communicate with them, teach them the household rules, and as a result establish a strong and immensely satisfying lifelong bond with them.

WHY TRAIN YOUR SHELTIE?

Shelties are intelligent dogs and have a well-deserved reputation for being easy to train. But what does it mean "to train" a dog?

Training is essentially a way to teach your dog what you want him to do and what you don't want him to do. It's important to realize that, whether you think you're training him or not, your Sheltie is always learning. It's your job to keep him from repeating, and thus learning, behaviors you don't find acceptable. More important, but too often neglected, it's your job to teach him to repeat behaviors that please you until they become habitual. Remember, "easy to train" does not mean that Shelties train themselves!

Seven Ways to Increase Your Training Success

As you train your Sheltie, remember this: Learning is hard work. Think about the last time you learned a new complex skill. Did you understand everything all at once? Did you make any mistakes? Now imagine that your teacher was a member of another species that communicates through a completely different means than human speech. That's pretty

Training gives your dog the confidence he needs to be a self-assured, mannerly companion and member of his community.

much the situation in which your Sheltie finds himself. Fortunately, he's somewhat prepared by thousands of years of canine evolution to learn to please you. More importantly, he wants to please you, and he loves you.

Keeping in mind that he's faced with this enormous challenge, you can apply seven basic training principles to make the process easier and more effective. A slip now and then won't hamper your dog's progress, but if you can follow these guidelines most of the time, your Sheltie will learn much more quickly and confidently:

- **Be consistent**: Use one command and/or signal to mean one action, and use a different command for each different action. Remember, human language is not natural to a dog, and he'll find it much easier to associate a sound (a word) with an action if the same one-to-one connection always applies. In addition, don't change the rules on him. If he's allowed on the couch one day and not the next, how can he learn what he's really supposed to do?

- **Be concise:** If you want your Sheltie to respond quickly to commands, tell him the command only once. If you repeat the command ("sit, sit, sit, sit, SIT"), what your dog will learn is that he doesn't have to respond until you tell him numerous times and your voice hits a certain volume.

- **Be generous:** Reward your Sheltie when he gets it right. The benefits of doing what you say may not be obvious to your dog unless you show him. We'll discuss how to do that later in this chapter.
- **Be smart:** When your dog is still learning—or relearning—don't give a command you can't enforce. If you do, he learns that he only has to obey sometimes.
- **Be prepared:** Know in advance what you will need to do to consistently reinforce a command. For example, don't stand on the back porch and call your dog ineffectively over and over again. Instead, keep a long line by the back door and use it to reel him in if he doesn't come the first time you call (and reward him when he gets to you).
- **Be cheerful:** Your dog is your friend, and you are training partners, not adversaries. Use a happy voice when you give commands and when you praise him. Dogs love and respond to happy human voices.
- **Be nonviolent:** Never hit your Sheltie—not with your hand, a rolled up newspaper, or anything at all. He won't learn what you want him to do by being physically punished. He will, however, learn that you can't be trusted. Use positive motivational reinforcement to tell him he's correct.

Positive Training

Training should not be just a means to an obedient dog, but also a way to build trust, mutual respect, and understanding between the two of you. Positive reinforcement—the process of rewarding your dog for correctly doing what you want him to do—is a wonderful way to accomplish that.

Again, it's your job to find out what works best for your dog. Professional trainers know that rewarding your dog for good behavior is the best way to motivate learning and that a training reward has to be something that your dog likes and wants. Food is highly motivating for many dogs, as are toys, butt scratches, and even a chance to run in circles. As his trainer, you need to figure out how to reward and motivate your Sheltie because every dog is an individual. If one type of reward doesn't catch his interest, try something else. When you find things that make him eager to learn, rotate them so he doesn't become bored.

Some trainers prefer purely positive training, meaning that they reward correct behaviors and ignore incorrect ones. Others combine positive reinforcement for correct behaviors and fair, gentle corrections for unwanted behaviors. In any case, punishment and rough handling have no place in dog training, especially with a dog as sensitive and willing to please as a Sheltie.

Always remember that your voice, body language, and attitude speak volumes to your dog. Dogs respond much better to a happy-sounding voice than to grumbles and growls, so pay attention to the tone of your commands, praise, and corrections. Try to pitch your voice high and keep the tone upbeat. Dogs are also very attuned to posture and movement. Try to be relaxed and confident whenever you interact with your Sheltie. Don't use threatening gestures or movements to intimidate your dog. Hitting, yelling, and frightening body language have no place in dog training.

GETTING OFF ON THE RIGHT PAW

Training begins as soon as you bring your Sheltie home, whether you mean it to or not, so be aware of what you communicate to your dog right from the start.

Whether he's a puppy or an adult, your Sheltie must learn the rules and routine of your household. Even if he has always been a house dog, the rules and routine in your home are undoubtedly a little different from those to which he was previously accustomed. He can't read your mind, so be patient and help him to learn what he needs to know to please you.

Special training words will be very useful in getting your Sheltie adjusted to life in his new home, so begin teaching them as soon as possible. First, you need to choose a praise word to tell your dog when he's done something correctly. Begin by saying the word whenever you give him a reward such as food or a toy. He will soon associate it with good things and understand that it means he's done well. Use a

Older Dogs *Can* Learn New Tricks!

It's never too late to begin or renew your Sheltie's obedience training. Adult dogs are able to focus longer than are puppies and usually enjoy the attention they get in training sessions. If your dog has had no previous training, it may take him a few sessions to understand what's expected, but once he "learns to learn," he'll no doubt be an eager student.

word your dog doesn't hear all the time. If, like most people, you tell him he's a good dog just for being there, don't use "good boy" for praise in training because it just won't mean much. I use "very nice!" or "excellent!" to praise my dogs.

Also teach your Sheltie a release word that tells him he can stop performing the behavior—he sat when you told him to, for instance, and the release word lets him know when he doesn't have to sit any longer. Although many trainers use "OK" to release their dogs, a word your dog doesn't hear in casual conversation will keep you from accidentally releasing him. "Free" or "go play" are good release words.

Establishing Household Rules

It's also important to decide on the household rules before you bring your Sheltie home. For example, is he allowed in the carpeted living room? On the couch? On the beds? By being clear and consistent about what you want right from the start, your dog will know what's expected of him and not be stressed by getting lots of mixed signals. Make sure all the members of the household know what the rules are. If your Sheltie is a puppy, think ahead to the adult behaviors you will expect. Don't let your puppy do things you won't want him to do later—that's confusing and unfair. If anything, your dog should gain privileges as he matures, not lose them. If you don't want your adult Sheltie to jump up on people, teach him not to do so as a puppy. If you don't want him to beg for food when he's older, don't feed him at the table while he's young. Bad habits are hard to break, so encourage lifelong good habits in your new dog.

Take advantage of opportunities as they come up to reinforce the behavioral habits you want your Sheltie to form. Training occurs all the time, not just during formal training sessions. However, those sessions are important, too, so plan two or three short sessions in which you focus on teaching or practicing one or two specific behaviors. Puppies have very short attention spans, but they learn very quickly, so several 5-minute training sessions on basic lessons such as sit, come, and down can be very productive. As your Sheltie matures, he'll be able to focus for longer periods, but even then 10- to 15-minute sessions two or three times a day are often more productive and less boring than one long one. And don't forget to include play in your training time! Learning is hard work, but there's no reason it can't also be fun.

SOCIALIZATION

Socialization is the process of introducing your Sheltie to the world and its inhabitants so that he is comfortable and confident throughout his life. Because Shelties tend by nature to be reserved, intensive socialization between the ages of seven and sixteen weeks is critical to your dog's ability to function to his fullest potential.

What do you need to do to "intensively socialize" your Sheltie? Ideally, you will take him out every single day from his seventh through sixteenth week so that he sees and, when possible to do so safely, interacts with people of all kinds: old, young, male, female, different races, bearded and clean shaven—the goal is to provide as much variety as possible. He also needs to meet other animals, especially nonaggressive dogs (follow your veterinarian's advice on balancing the need for socialization with the need to protect him from disease before he is fully vaccinated).

Your puppy should also experience as many sights and sounds as possible, and walk on as many different safe surfaces as you can provide: city sidewalks, paths in the woods, sand, boardwalks, and so on. The more he experiences by the time he's four months old, the more confident he will be in the face of new things later in life. Be cautious during the fear period that occurs around the eighth week (see "The Best Time to Bring Your Puppy Home" in Chapter 3), but continue to expose him to things that won't be frightening. The socialization process should continue throughout puberty and young adulthood, but needn't be as intensive as during the first four months.

It's important to socialize your dog to all types of people, other dogs and animals, and different environments.

Keeping Children Safe Around Dogs

No matter how reliable you think your Sheltie is, all interaction between your dog and children should be supervised by a responsible adult who can intervene immediately if necessary, especially when your dog and/or child are young. Children often react to rough puppy play by screaming, jumping around, pushing the puppy away, and getting excited, which your pup may interpret as play or as scary and dangerous. Dog and child interactions can get out of control very quickly, and both participants can end up frightened, injured, or both. Always exercise caution, and never leave youngsters and dogs alone together.

CRATE TRAINING

A crate is one of the best tools available for training your puppy or new dog. Used properly, it will keep your dog and your belongings safe as your Sheltie learns to be a well-mannered canine companion. Moreover, if you use the crate as it's meant to be used, your dog will consider it his den and may even choose to go there on his own at times.

Introducing the Crate

If your Sheltie has never been crated prior to joining your family, he may complain about being locked in at first. Don't give in! If you let him out when he barks or whines, he will learn that noise makes you open the crate. Tough it out until he quiets down—he will eventually—and then reward him with a treat while he's still in the crate. Don't reward him after you let him out because you want him to associate being inside the crate with the good stuff. Freedom is it's own reward as well, so once he has calmed down, you can let him out if you want to do so.

It's also important to remember that your Sheltie should always think of his crate as a good, safe place, so never use it for punishment. However, tired puppies, like human babies, sometimes act cranky and wild and can be put to bed for a while.

Crate Requirements

Shelties vary greatly in size, but generally a crate about 16 by 20 inches (41 by 51 cm) is a good fit. If your dog is at the large or

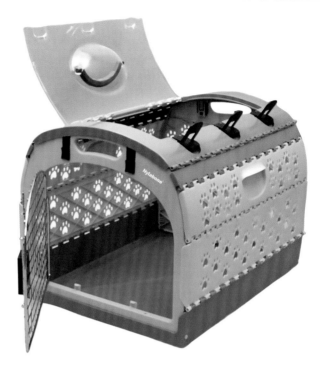

A crate is one of the best tools available for training your puppy or new dog.

small extremes of Sheltie size, the basic rule of thumb is that he should be able to stand up, turn around, and lie down easily in his crate. If you're housetraining a puppy, you may want to use a smaller crate than your dog will need as an adult, or block off part of an adult-sized crate to limit the usable space. Healthy dogs raised in clean surroundings don't like to sleep where they potty, so a sleeping-room-only crate will eliminate that option and help the housetraining process be more effective, as long as you're sure to take your puppy out regularly and often.

Many dogs like to sleep on soft bedding, but if your pup isn't yet potty trained, leave the bedding out. You don't want anything inside the crate that will absorb urine. Never use weewee pads (which are impregnated with a hormone that tells the puppy "pee here") as crate liners. If your Sheltie is prone to ripping things to shreds, leave the bedding out as well.

Adjusting to the Crate

To teach your dog to go into his crate willingly, don't shove him in by force. Instead, toss in a treat or a special chew toy that he gets only in the crate, tell him, "Crate" or "Kennel," and praise him when he gets inside it. Leave the door open sometimes, and quietly close it at other times. Always give your puppy something to do while he's crated. Playing with a safe chew toy, such as a Nylabone, is a good choice. Never give him anything he can break apart and swallow. Feed him his meals in his crate, at least for a while, so he knows it's a wonderful place. If possible, put your pup's crate in your bedroom at night. He'll sleep longer and more quietly if he knows he's with his "pack."

Length of Confinement

How long should your dog be crated? The general recommendation for a puppy is no more hours than his age in months plus one; for example, if your puppy is two months old, three hours is the maximum time he should spend in a crate (except at night when he's sleeping). Older dogs can manage several hours, but it's really unfair to make being crated for long hours (more than four) a routine part of your dog's life.

If you must be gone all day, make arrangements for your Sheltie's comfort in advance. It's not fair to make a puppy spend eight or nine hours alone. It's even worse to expect him to wait to go potty for that long or, if he can't, to lie in his own urine or feces. If necessary, hire a reliable pet sitter or dog walker to take your pup out once or twice during the day. If you can't make suitable arrangements, an adult Sheltie is a better choice than a puppy.

HOUSETRAINING

You probably agree with most other dog owners that housetraining is the first and most important kind of training a dog needs. Fortunately, Shelties are usually fairly easy to housetrain, as long as their people are alert and consistent. If you take your puppy out when he needs to potty, and respond calmly when he has an accident, your Sheltie should understand where to eliminate and where not to in short order. If your new Sheltie is an adult who was never been housetrained, the procedures that follow apply as well, with the added advantage that, assuming he's healthy, your mature dog has better control.

Prevention and Patience

The two most important principles of housetraining are prevention and patience. If you're training a puppy, remember that he's a baby, and even if he wants to control his bladder and bowels he may not be able to yet. By the time he realizes that he has to potty, he may not be able to wait until he's outdoors. It's your job—not his—to limit his activity to easily cleaned surfaces and to help him make it to the right spot so that he can learn where he should potty.

Given a chance to develop clean habits, most puppies do signal when they're about to go, so when your pup is loose in the house, watch him closely. If he starts to turn in circles, sniff the floor, or hunch his back while walking, pick him up and take him out. Don't expect him to always make it out the door once he knows he needs to potty. Help him do the right thing.

Typically, a puppy will need to go:

- after every meal
- first thing in the morning
- last thing at night
- whenever he wakes up
- after or during active play
- in the middle of the night, especially when he's very young

Whatever his age, teach your Sheltie where you want him to eliminate, put him on leash, and take him to the right spot. Don't play with him until he's finished; just stand and wait. You can teach him to go on command by using a specific word or expression whenever he starts to go, such as "hurry up." Eventually, you'll be able to speed up potty breaks by taking him out and telling him to "hurry up." When he's finished, praise him and give him a treat or a short playtime session. Wait a few minutes before you take him in, though—puppies don't always do everything right away, so give him time to be sure he won't need to go again in three minutes. Besides, you don't want him to learn to hold it so he can stay out longer. If he doesn't go within 10 minutes, crate him for 10 to 15 minutes, then take him out again.

Dealing With Accidents

If your Sheltie does soil the floor (why wasn't someone watching him?), you need to remove all trace of odor from that spot. Remember, his nose works much better than yours, and he can detect very small traces of urine or feces, which announce "go here." Regular cleaners aren't enough; you need to use a special cleanser designed to eliminate odors, usually ones that contain

When housetraining your Sheltie, choose a spot in your yard where you want him to eliminate and take him to that same area every time.

enzymes. For urine odors (but not feces), you can also use an inexpensive 50/50 mixture of white vinegar and water.

If your dog has an accident, do not punish him or yell at him, and definitely don't rub his nose in it. Those methods are abusive, and they won't help him learn. In fact, they often cause the dog to go where you can't see him in order to avoid the abuse. If you must punish someone, roll up a newspaper and whack yourself in the noggin a few times for not helping your dog do the right thing. Understand, too, that your Sheltie won't poop on the carpet to annoy you or get even with you. If he does it at all, it will be because he has to go and hasn't yet learned how to ask you to let him out. Take a deep breath (maybe not too deep!), take your dog out in case he isn't finished, clean up, and supervise him more closely until he's reliable.

Paper Training

What about paper training, you ask? If you want your Sheltie to potty outdoors as an adult, why train him to go indoors—even on papers—as a pup? The only time paper training might be a good idea is if you really have to leave your pup in the house for long hours. In that case, fence off an area with an easily cleaned bare floor, give him a play and sleeping area at one end and fresh water that he can't spill, and make a small area of newspapers or weewee pads.

Housetraining Tips

Here are a few other tips to make housetraining go smoothly:
- Feed your Sheltie a high-quality dry food so that his stools will be smaller and more compact and his bowels easier to control.
- Don't give your Sheltie the run of the house until he's reliably housetrained. Keep him in the room you're in, and watch him closely.
- Maintain a regular feeding schedule, and try to get up and go to bed on a regular schedule until he's reliably housetrained.
- During housetraining, feed your Sheltie at least four hours before bedtime, and remove his water two hours before bedtime.
- Keep your Sheltie's potty place free of feces. He doesn't want to step in it any more than you do.

It can take several months for a puppy or some older dogs to be completely reliable, although many Shelties learn much faster than that. However, certain medical problems can make it difficult or impossible for a dog to maintain control. If your Sheltie is still having frequent accidents in the house at six months or older, or after a reasonable training period, or if he loses his housetraining after being reliable, talk to your veterinarian.

LEASH TRAINING

Knowing how to walk politely on a leash is essential if your Sheltie and you are to go out together safely. Like most herding dogs, Shelties have a tendency to literally run circles around people, and your dog needs to learn not to do that when on leash so that you don't end up hog tied or tripped.

The first step in leash training is to be sure your dog's collar fits securely and properly and that his leash is long enough to give him reasonable freedom of movement but not so long that it's hard to manage. If you're training a puppy, or if your adult Sheltie is responsive and submissive to you, try the "no forward progress" response to pulling first: If your dog pulls, stop and stand still until he stops pulling. It may take him a few attempts to notice that whenever he pulls you stop moving, but

Having the right tools, such as a properly fitting collar and leash, can make training your dog easier and more effective.

he will. When he stops pulling, praise him and resume walking. If he pulls again, halt. Your Sheltie will soon realize that pulling is counterproductive, while polite walking keeps him moving. When he seems to understand this concept more reliably, begin to say "Easy" or "Don't pull" as you halt. If you do this consistently, he'll soon stop pulling whenever you tell him to and you'll no longer have to stop.

To teach your Sheltie not to run around you in circles, begin by giving him less leash. As he walks nicely beside you, occasionally praise him and give him a little treat. If he seems to settle into his proper place at your side (the left side is traditional), give him a little more leash. If he starts to circle again, shorten your leash. Remember that your dog is fighting instinct here, and he doesn't realize that the leash makes his antics dangerous, so be patient and don't expect him to learn immediately. Eventually, though, if you're consistent, he'll get the idea.

GOING TO DOGGY SCHOOL

You'll do most of your Sheltie's training at home or out and about because that's where the two of you will spend most of your time. Although good training books and articles will certainly help you improve your training skills, they can't replace the benefits of a good obedience class taught by a qualified instructor who actually teaches *you* to train your dog. A good class also gives your Sheltie—and you—a chance to socialize with dogs and the people who love them, and it offers you a supportive environment in which you can work out training problems that you find especially challenging.

Puppy Kindergarten

If your Sheltie is a young pup, a puppy kindergarten class will be particularly useful for socializing him and beginning obedience training. Puppy kindergarten classes usually meet once a week for four to eight weeks, but you'll also have to practice at home. Sheltie puppies are smart little cookies and can quickly learn basic commands such as *sit, down, come,* and *stay,* as well as other skills that form the foundation for more advanced training later. Just remember to keep the training fun and each training session short. And don't demand perfection from a puppy. After all, he's not just learning new skills, he's learning about human language and how to take direction from you, which is hard work!

Basic Obedience Class

For an older puppy or dog, or a puppy who has graduated from puppy kindergarten, a basic obedience class that teaches good manners and promotes social skills is usually the best next step. If you plan to eventually take up canine sports with your Sheltie, look for an instructor who understands your goals. Early training should provide a foundation for advanced training, and ideally your instructor will help you and your dog avoid habits that you will later have to unlearn. Young dogs shouldn't perform strenuous activities—jumping, weaving through poles, and similar things—until their bones and joints mature, but they can certainly learn to pay attention and follow directions.

Beware of any instructor who promises that your dog will be completely trained in a few weeks. As in other areas of life, if the promise seems too good to be true . . . well, you know. Obedience and other kinds of training should be aimed at building advanced skills on a firm foundation, as well as in building trust and understanding between dog and owner. Always remember that you are your Sheltie's protector. If you are uncomfortable with anything an instructor asks you to do with your dog, don't do it. Be very cautious about who you allow to handle your dog. Intimidation and harsh methods are unnecessary and have no place in your Sheltie's education. Look for an instructor who uses positive, motivational training methods.

FOUR COMMANDS YOUR SHELTIE SHOULD KNOW

Come, sit, down, and *stay*: These four commands are essential, and even puppies can learn them. The following section explains one way to teach each of these commands. Remember, though, that there are many ways to train any behavior. Taking at least one obedience class will benefit both you and your Sheltie, and reading books and articles written by professional trainers will expand your understanding of various positive training techniques.

No single method works for every dog or person, so if one isn't working for you, evaluate what you're doing to be sure you're giving your dog clear direction. If you think you are, look for an alternate method that may work better for both you and your dog. If necessary, take another obedience class. You're dog isn't the only one who is learning—you are, too—and there's nothing wrong with taking a refresher course.

Come

One of the most important things you can teach your Sheltie is to come immediately when you call him. Not only is a dog who comes reliably when called less frustrating or worrisome for whoever is calling him, but he's also safer. Not coming when called away from danger can get your Sheltie injured or killed.

Teaching your dog to come when called is not really difficult. And yet most of the pet dogs you know don't come when their people call, do they? That's because people frequently teach their dogs to ignore them. So let's begin with a few ground rules to keep you from training your Sheltie to ignore the *come* command:

- Always let your Sheltie know that coming to you is a safe and wonderful thing to do. When you call your dog, he should come running because he knows that you are calling him to the most fun place he could possibly be. Teach him this by always being overjoyed when he gets to you. Never call him to you for anything he finds unpleasant, and never punish him for anything after calling him to you.

- Always praise your dog for coming when you call, and from time to time reward him as well with a treat, toy, belly rub— something he likes.
- Always be consistent about the word you use to call your dog. Common commands are *come* or *here*, but the word itself doesn't matter. Just don't confuse your dog with changing commands (*come, come here, here, get over here, you better get your butt over here,* etc.).
- Never repeat the command; that simply teaches your dog to ignore you. If he doesn't come when you call, go get him and put him on leash. Then call him once and pull him in with the leash. When he gets to you, praise him and reward him for coming.
- Never let your Sheltie off leash in an unfenced area if he doesn't come on the first command every single time he's called. That means he comes to you even if there are distractions such as squirrels, other dogs, motorcycles, kids eating cookies, or whatever. Even if you believe your dog is reliable, and even if it's legal to let him off leash, be extremely cautious. A single failure to come when called could get your beautiful Sheltie injured or killed. Leashes save lives.
- Never call your dog when you can't enforce the command (like when you're standing in the doorway wrapped in a towel!) until you believe he is reliable. He is reliable when he has developed the habit of coming immediately the first time you call him, *every* time you call him. If you can't trust your dog to come when you call, put him on a leash or long line when he goes out to potty. If you jump the gun and find that he's not as reliable as you thought, start over. If he learns that he must always obey, eventually he won't think of not obeying—most of the time, at least! If you call him over and over, he learns that you don't mean what you say and he doesn't have to come.

Teaching the Come Command

Your Sheltie can learn the *come* command at any age. Very young puppies can learn to come when called, and so can older dogs, even those who have been taught to ignore the *come* command. One helpful suggestion, though: If your dog has previously learned to ignore your word for "come," find a new word and use it for retraining. "Here" is commonly used, and I have heard trainers use more unusual commands such as "by

Come is the single most important command you can teach your dog. A dog who doesn't come when called can become lost or injured.

me" and "find me." The important thing is not the command word itself but what your Sheltie understands it to mean.

To begin, start with your puppy or dog on leash, or in a very small room or fenced area so that he's safe and can't wander very far away. Hold a toy he likes or a small, yummy treat. Say "Lassie, come!" *only one time* in a happy, playful voice. Do whatever you have to do, but do not repeat the command to get your dog to come to you—act silly, walk or run the other way, crouch down, play with the toy, etc. If he absolutely won't come on his own, gently pull him in with the leash. If he starts to come on his own after you pull, great: stop pulling. If not, gently reel him in. When he gets to you, whether on his own or with a little help, praise and reward him. Let him know how happy he's made you. Then let him return to whatever he was doing before you called. Repeat the process two or three times, then quit. Do this several times a day if possible.

If you're not the only human in the household, make a group game of teaching your dog to come. Call him back and forth or from one person to another. Just make sure that only one person calls at a time and that each person rewards him for coming. And make sure that everyone understands the importance of being consistent with this training.

Sit

Sit is the one command that almost all dogs seem to know, at

Basic obedience commands like the sit-stay *are the foundation for good manners and all future learning.*

least part of the time. Somehow dogs who don't obey any other command will happily plunk their fannies down when anyone says "Sit." Why is that? Because people frequently reward their dogs for sitting by giving them food, they are always being trained for this behavior. Even dogs who don't sit on command on walks or at obedience class are happy sitters in the kitchen. The lesson for all would-be dog trainers? Teach your dog that there's a very good chance he'll get a goodie if he does what you say. Once he's learned a command, you don't need to give him a treat every time. In fact, it's better if you don't as long as you give him something he likes once in a while. Rather like people feeding coins into slot machines, dogs will perform as directed if there's the hope of a reward.

Sit is a very useful command. It gives you control of your dog. When he's doing something you don't want him to do, like jumping up on people, telling him to sit gives him an appropriate alternative. And if you plan to compete in obedience or agility, a good *sit* response is essential.

Teaching the Sit Command

Start with your dog on leash or confined in a small space. Hold a small treat in front of his nose, but don't let him take it. When your dog shows interest, *slowly* move your treat hand up and back over his head. As he raises his head up to follow the treat, his rear end has to go down. (Warning: If you lift the treat too high, he'll probably jump for it or just be confused, so keep it within a few inches [cm] of his head.) When your dog begins to lower his fanny to sit down, say "Sit." The moment his fanny hits the floor, praise him and give him the treat. Make sure you give him the treat while he is sitting. If he stands back up before you give it to him, have him sit again and be quicker giving him the treat. You want him to learn right from the start that when you tell him to do something, he's to do it promptly and continue doing it until you tell him he can stop. To teach him to hold the *sit,* use your release word before he stands up to tell him when he can stop sitting. Repeat three or four times, then quit for a while.

When your dog sits promptly every time you say "Sit," you can begin training him to sit for a longer period of time by having him continue to sit after giving him the treat and gradually extending the time he holds the sit before you release him. Later in the training, you can wean away the treat most of the time and reward him with praise and play after you release him. Eventually, he should sit on the first command and stay sitting without another command until you tell him he's off duty. (In open, intermediate-level obedience competition, dogs have to sit for three minutes while their handlers leave them and go out of sight.)

Down

Down (or *lie down*) is another very useful command, and it gives you even more control than the *sit* command does. Most people teach their dogs to lie down from a sit, but I like to teach the *down* command from a stand for several reasons. The main reason is that it eliminates an intermediate step. Also, if you plan to compete with your dog in many sports, including obedience, agility, herding, and even tracking, there are times when your dog will need to lie down from a stand or even while moving. It's much easier to teach those maneuvers if your Sheltie doesn't think he has to sit before he lies down. If he's already trained to lie down from a sit, and you want to teach him to lie down from a stand or while moving, a different command may make it easier—maybe *drop* or *crash,* for instance.

A note about terminology: Although most experienced trainers use *down* for "Lie down," and *off* for "Don't jump up" or "Get off the couch," many people use *down* to mean "Get off." If you are one of them, find another word to mean "Lie down." Remember, a command should have only one meaning. *Settle* is one possible alternative.

Teaching the Down *Command*

Start with your dog standing beside or in front of you. At first, you may want to kneel to make it easier. Hold a treat and slowly move your hand downward under your dog's chin, toward his front legs, lowering it more as you go. As his head follows the treat, he should fold himself into a down position. If he bows instead of lying down, gently guide his rear end down. If he steps back instead of lying down, try moving your hand more slowly. If that doesn't work, hold your other hand behind him so that he can't back up. If he lowers his head but doesn't lie down, press very gently between his shoulder blades to guide him. If he still doesn't go down, don't try to force him. Keep the treat close to the ground with one hand, and cradle his hind legs from behind with the other, gently tightening your arm around his hind legs until he folds down. Then praise and reward him.

When your Sheltie responds to the moving treat by folding quickly backward into a down position, add your command, telling him "Down" (or your other word) as you begin. When he's doing that quickly and reliably, give him the command but don't move your hand toward him. When he lies down, praise and reward him. Be sure to give him the treat while he's lying down, not after he gets up. As with the *sit* command, slowly increase the length of time he has to stay down before he gets the treat.

Stay

The *stay* command tells your dog not to move from whatever place and position he's in until you release him. The down position is the easiest for your Sheltie to hold without moving, so teach *stay* first with the *down*. If he learns the concept of staying where he is when down, he'll find it easier to learn to stay when sitting or standing.

Teaching the Stay Command

Have your dog lie down and tell him "Stay." If he starts to get up, put him back in the down position and tell him to stay again. When he has stayed down for a few seconds, praise, reward, and release him, *in that order*. If you reward him after he gets up, you're teaching him to get up, not to stay. Start with very short stays—less than a minute—and remain close to your dog. Increase the time very slowly—a few seconds a day, and only when he stays reliably—until he will stay five minutes with you standing close to him.

When your dog is reliable for a few seconds with you right there, tell him "Down" and "Stay," and take one step away from him. Have him stay for thirty seconds, then step close to him and praise, reward, and release him. Build the time up slowly to five minutes. Repeat this process as you increase distance, reducing the length of time and building it back up again every time you add distance. If your dog starts popping up, fidgeting, or whining before the time is up, stand a little closer for a few days until he's comfortable and reliable. Then proceed to add more time and distance.

The biggest mistake that people make when teaching the *stay* command is to increase the time and distance too quickly. If your dog is getting up before you release him, you have passed his comfort level. Reduce the time and shorten your distance from him until he is reliable, then slowly increase them again.

Practice *down-stays* in different environments so that your Sheltie learns to stay anywhere you issue the command. Make sure you have control of the location; for example, if you practice in a park alive with squirrels, keep your dog on a leash or long line. You can practice stays at home while you're doing other things, but don't neglect to come back and release him in an appropriate amount of time. You need to give and cancel commands reliably if you want your dog to obey them.

When your Sheltie stays reliably for five minutes when he's lying down, repeat the training process with him sitting. Don't cut corners on time and distance—a *sit-stay* and a *down-stay* may seem similar to you, but they are different to your dog. Take your time building time and distance. A solid foundation for these commands at this stage of training will save you a lot of frustration and remedial training later.

GETTING A GRIP ON PROBLEM BEHAVIORS

With careful planning and quick responses, you can prevent or eliminate most problem behaviors. We'll look at some of the most common ones in a moment. First, though, here are some general practices and principles that will help you keep your Sheltie from developing bad habits and help you "reform" them if he does:

- Why is your dog doing what he's doing? Is he responding to his instinct? Is he bored and full of energy? Have you accidentally rewarded him for doing something you don't really want him to do? Look at both your dog's behavior and your response to it.
- Has your Sheltie trained you instead of the other way around? Do you hand him a biscuit when he stares at you and barks? Don't be embarrassed; plenty of people are trained by their smart dogs. Once you catch on, though, it's time to turn the tables. Either ignore your Sheltie's demands (he'll give up

Once problem behaviors are identified, they can usually be controlled or eliminated. For example, to prevent digging, supervise your dog when he is outdoors.

eventually if you absolutely never give in), or require him to do something to earn what he wants.

- Give your dog an acceptable alternative. It's much easier to teach him to do *something* than to do *nothing*. If he takes your slipper, take it from him and give him a dog toy. If he jumps on you, have him sit or lie down.
- Be proactive about preventing unwanted behaviors. If your Sheltie is not yet reliably housetrained, don't give him the run of the house and leave him unsupervised (see also, "Crate Training" and "Housetraining"). If he digs up your pansies when he's alone in the yard, don't leave him alone in the yard. In other words, set your dog and your training program up for success, not failure.
- Three words: exercise, exercise, exercise! Channel that famous Sheltie energy into safe activities. Shelties are high-energy dogs, so give your canine companion problems to solve. He needs to use his intelligence or he'll be bored, and boredom leads to trouble. Advanced training in obedience, agility, herding, tracking, and other activities can relieve boredom and use up energy. Even if you don't want to compete, you can train in one or more of these activities for fun. You can also invent little games to make him think (hide the cookie, for instance) or teach him to perform parlor tricks to dazzle your friends and family.
- Educate your Sheltie. Basic obedience training not only helps build trust and understanding between dog and owner, but usually results in better behavior across the board.

Now lets look at some specific behaviors in which most people don't want their dogs to indulge.

Aggression

True aggression is not normal, and a dog who threatens to bite, tries to bite, or does bite is potentially dangerous to people and other pets. Don't underestimate the ability of a Sheltie to cause a serious injury. A dog's small size doesn't mean he can't be dangerous. If your Sheltie growls or bares his teeth at you or any other member of your family, snaps, or guards his food, toys, bed, or anything else from you or other people, get qualified professional help immediately. Don't ignore aggression in the hope that it will get better on its own. It won't. If your Sheltie is aggressive, or if you're not sure whether his

behavior is normal, get help from a dog trainer or behaviorist who is qualified to deal with this very serious problem. In the meantime, don't take any chances, especially if you have children.

Aggression in dogs can be caused by a number of factors. Some dogs simply have unstable or aggressive temperaments, some have been taught to behave aggressively, and certain medical problems can also cause aggressive behavior.

Solution

Your first response to aggressive behavior should be to take your Sheltie to the vet for a thorough physical examination. Explain exactly what's going on so that she knows what to look for. Your vet may recommend certain tests to check for specific medical problems. If a physical reason for the aggression can be identified, it may be possible to treat it medically.

Altering reduces aggression in both males and females, especially if it's done before the dog reaches sexual maturity, so if your Sheltie isn't already spayed or neutered, consider having the surgery done as soon as possible.

Your next step is to work with a professional trainer or behaviorist to determine whether the problem can be solved through behavior modification. You can get a referral from your vet or breeder, or from the Association of Pet Dog Trainers (APDT) website at www.apdt.com.

Some people insist that aggression can be fixed if you just do the right things. Unfortunately, that's not always true. Some dogs can be rehabilitated through medical or behavioral intervention, but some cannot. Here's the bottom line: No matter why your dog is aggressive, and no matter how much you love him, if you cannot guarantee that he will *never* injure any person or pet without reasonable provocation, then the most responsible thing to do may be to have him humanely euthanized. That is a difficult, sad, and painful decision to have to make, but sometimes it is the most loving thing you can do. You can discuss this option with your vet if you feel that it may be a last resort.

Anxiety or Fear

Separation anxiety is an all too common condition in which a dog becomes worried and agitated in his owner's absence. A dog with separation anxiety may exhibit any or all of a range of

Fair Warning

Although people often claim that a dog bit them "without warning," that rarely happens. The trouble is that many people, especially children, don't notice or understand canine warning signals, or don't take them seriously. Even worse, some people think a growling dog is funny. It's not, and neither is a bite. If your Sheltie's hair stands on end (especially along his spine), or if he stands with his legs still and his tail straight up, or if he growls and bares his teeth, he's telling you to back off as clearly as he knows how. If your Sheltie shows any warning signals without legitimate reason, don't wait until he bites someone. Get help immediately from your veterinarian or a qualified canine behaviorist.

behaviors, including whining, barking, howling, pacing the floor, running in circles, drooling, vomiting, and inappropriate urination or defecation. Some dogs chew things they shouldn't, including sometimes themselves. The severity of the anxiety varies from barely noticeable behavioral changes that suggest mild worry to extreme agitation and behavior that is hazardous to property and to the dog himself.

Solution

If your Sheltie exhibits signs of separation anxiety, you must keep him safe and prevent him from damaging property or disturbing your neighbors when you're gone. If you don't already have one, get a crate and train your dog to be comfortable in it (see "Crate Training"). Have him spend some time in his crate while you're home so he won't associate the crate strictly with your absence. Locate the crate where it will help ease his anxiety; your bedroom, which smells like you, may be a good spot. Voices or music help some dogs relax, so try leaving a radio or television on with the volume turned down low. Be sure to tune to a station that won't disturb him with yelling and loud, banging sounds. Some dogs also calm down when they can snuggle something that smells like their people; try an old sweatshirt that you haven't laundered since you last wore it. However, if your Sheltie is prone to chewing or ripping things up, don't give him anything that can hurt him. He'll soon see his crate as a safe little den, whether you're at home or away.

People also often create or contribute to separation anxiety by their own behavior when leaving and arriving home. Shelties are very sensitive to the emotions of those around them. How can your dog not worry about your absence if you act as if leaving is so sad and coming home is such a joyous relief? To avoid creating or reinforcing that impression, put your dog in his crate ten to fifteen minutes before you plan to leave so that he can relax while you go about your business. Give him a special chew toy that he likes but gets only when you're gone. If you have a puppy, you'll need to get him out to potty as soon as you come home, but do it calmly, without making a big fuss. If your Sheltie is older, he can wait a few minutes while you change clothes, check your answering machine, whatever. Let him calm down and get

To prevent separation anxiety, make sure your dog has a variety of toys to play with when he is alone.

used to your being home before you let him out, and again, when you do, don't make a big fuss.

Try to figure out how soon your dog becomes anxious after you leave the room or your house, and begin reconditioning him. To do this, put him in his crate, calmly leave the room or the house, wait, then come back. If he's calm when you return, quietly praise him and reward him with a little treat, then let him out of the crate. If he's agitated, stay nearby but ignore him until he relaxes. Begin with very short practice periods several times a day, and slowly increase the time you stay away as he improves. Regardless of how long you need to be away, always use the same calm method of returning. Even if you can't stay home for a month to help train your dog to overcome his fears, you can reduce his worries by teaching him that no matter how long you're gone, nothing bad will happen to him while you're away, and you will come back.

If you haven't yet taken your Sheltie to an obedience class, now is the time. Basic obedience training using positive, motivational methods will help build your anxious dog's confidence. If his separation anxiety doesn't seem to improve, talk to your veterinarian or a qualified animal behaviorist. They may have suggestions relevant to your specific situation. In extreme cases, your vet may recommend anti-anxiety medication, but drugs are not a good long-term solution. Some people also report success with herbs, flower essences, and other unconventional treatments. Most of them won't hurt your dog, but there's no scientific proof that they work either. The best cure is patience and reconditioning to build your dog's trust and confidence.

Barking

No two ways about it: Most Shelties love to bark. Their ancestors were valued in part for their ability to warn their farm families of strangers and other potential concerns. More importantly, their jobs in the remote Shetland Islands included driving foraging livestock away from the labor-intensive gardens that provided food for the long, harsh winters, and sometimes to gather and herd those animals from one location to another. Their small stature made it difficult for the wee dogs to intimidate determined livestock with just their physical presence, as larger herding dogs would do, so they got results—and still do—largely with their voices and quick movements.

Even when there are no errant farm animals to deal with, barking is a natural means of communication for a dog. He barks to greet his friends, to warn others away, or to invite a playmate. Some dogs seem to bark for the pleasure of hearing their own voices. When they interact with people, dogs quickly discover that barking often gets them to do or provide certain things. Even as puppies, they learn to bark to go out, to come in, to initiate play, and to get attention. And, of course, your Sheltie will bark for some of the same reasons his ancestors did: a stranger at the door, a dog walking past the house, a squirrel on the bird feeder, and the like.

Most people tolerate a reasonable amount of canine vocal activity, but if your Sheltie barks frequently and for long periods, you and your neighbors will probably not be amused. Unless you live far from other people, you need to find a way to reduce the noise level, and that can be a challenge with a Sheltie. In the meantime, let your neighbors know that you're trying to solve the problem. Until the excessive barking is under control, don't leave your dog outdoors or in the house with the windows open when you're not at home, and when you are at home, don't let him stay outside barking for long periods.

Solution

Barking is a tough behavior to change, especially in a breed prone to barking. Many Sheltie breeders and owners give up and either live with the noise or have their dogs surgically "debarked," a procedure in which the vocal cords are cut. As you might suspect, the procedure is controversial. Some people find it cruel. Supporters of the practice contend that because the dog can still bark in a "whisper" it is less cruel to debark a dog than to yell or physically correct him, squirt water in his face, or put an electronic "no bark collar" on him. Whether you like the idea of debarking a dog or not, if an incorrigible barker is in danger of losing his home if he doesn't lose his voice, the surgical solution may be the best alternative. First, though, try to curtail your Sheltie's barking through less drastic methods.

Try to figure out if anything other than his heritage is encouraging your Sheltie to bark too much. Is he bored or overflowing with energy? Does he spend a lot of time alone? Do sights and sounds around your home and yard excite him so that he barks? Sometimes knowing the reason behind the barking leads to a fairly simple solution. Increasing your Sheltie's daily exercise may help. If he hasn't had basic obedience training, or hasn't practiced obedience skills in a while, an obedience class and regular practice sessions may help improve his behavior. Learning gives him something to think about and directs his activity toward positive alternatives.

Your Sheltie may be barking to alert you to "intruders." If he has spotted a burglar skulking around your garage, or a flock of sheep eating your hosta plants, good for him. But if he announces every neighbor who takes out the garbage and every bird that flies by, he's too enthusiastic about his watchdog duties. Again, obedience training may help by giving you a simple way to direct your dog away from unwanted behaviors. For example, when your Sheltie starts to bark at someone, have him sit or lie down and stay. If necessary, put his leash on so that he has to pay attention to you. When he's quiet, praise him and reward him.

Additional socialization may also help, as well as introductions to your neighbors; teaching your dog that neighbors and their pets are not threatening to you or to him will help him overcome this overprotective tendency. To train your Sheltie to respond appropriately, have a neighbor or a friend walk by your yard while you're there with him (on leash, if necessary, for control). If he is quiet, praise him and give him a treat. If he barks, have him lie down and stay, and praise and reward him as soon as he's quiet. Repeat the process several times a day for several days, having the "intruder" come closer as your dog becomes quieter and more steady on the stay. Try to enlist the help of different people so that he can generalize the quiet principle to whoever walks by.

The same procedure will also work for "window barkers." The key to success is consistency; don't ignore the barking one time, encourage it the next, and then yell at your dog the time after that. When you won't be home to respond to your Sheltie's barking, confine him to his crate or to an area of the house where he has no window from which to look out. You will probably never completely stop his barking, but you may be able to control it.

Some people turn to modern electronics for a solution to excessive barking. Bark collars (or more accurately "don't bark collars") are sold in discount stores as well as pet supply stores, and their makers promise an instantaneous end to problem

Dogs can easily become chronic barkers due to boredom and lack of attention.

barking. The collars are supposed to discourage barking by administering an electrical shock, a spray of citronella aimed at the dog's nose, or a high-pitched sound when a sensor detects vibration of the dog's vocal cords. The collars do seem to work sometimes, but they treat the symptoms rather than the cause. If your Sheltie barks because he's bored, he's likely to replace the barking with another undesirable behavior, such as digging or chewing. If he barks because he's anxious or afraid, a bark collar will increase his stress level and, again, lead to more neurotic behaviors. If he's territorial or aggressive, the discomfort caused by the collar may make him attack the person or animal he sees as the source of his discomfort. Finally, bark collars just don't work on some determined barkers. I've seen dogs with electrical burns from a collar's contacts still barking through the pain. Prevention, control, and training are the best way to turn down the volume.

Barking is sometimes symptomatic of other behavioral issues that have to be dealt with before you can reduce the barking itself. Dogs with separation anxiety, very territorial dogs, dogs who are fearful due to poor temperament or lack of socialization are often very reactive to stimuli and prone to barking at anyone or anything. (Fear or stress may also push some of these dogs to bite, by the way, so be cautious if your Sheltie falls into this category.) Again, basic obedience training may help by building your dog's confidence and giving you a better way to structure his life and behavior. If you have a dog who habitually overreacts to situations and stimuli, though, seek professional help.

Chewing

For your Sheltie, chewing on a nice raw knuckle bone or safe chew toy is the equivalent of reading a good book, knitting, or playing a computer game. Chewing relieves stress, dispels boredom, and feels good. While a puppy is cutting new teeth, chewing eases discomfort. So, chewing in itself is not a bad behavior. It becomes a problem only when your Sheltie chews the wrong things, wrecking your possessions and potentially causing himself harm. Smart as he is, your Sheltie was not born knowing what he's allowed to chew and what is off limits. You have to teach him that.

Although many adult dogs love a good chew, puppies and adolescents are especially prone to chewing anything they can fit into their mouths. Your puppy's deciduous (baby) teeth arrived when he was about four weeks old. At four to five months old, those "starter teeth" loosen, fall out, and are replaced by permanent (adult) teeth. His gums become swollen and sore, and to ease the discomfort and help the process of losing and replacing teeth, he needs to chew things.

If your Sheltie gnaws on your favorite things, try replacing them with a safe chew toy.

Solution

As with other problem behaviors, the best way to put an end to destructive or dangerous chewing is through prevention. First, put anything you don't want your Sheltie to chew out of his reach. Make sure your kids to do the same; small toys, especially those with tiny pieces like plastic eyeballs, do nothing good for the inside of a puppy's digestive system.

Teach your Sheltie that he's allowed to chew some things, but not everything. If he picks up something he shouldn't, take it from him gently and give him one of his toys. Don't yell, chase, or punish him; that won't teach him what's right and may lead to other unwanted behaviors. Encourage him to bring things he shouldn't have to you by praising him and rewarding him, and when you take something away, always give him something else in return. Think about the things you give him to play with, too. How is he to tell the difference between an old shoe you allow him to gnaw on and your brand spankin' new ones? They all smell like you—wonderful! Think ahead, be consistent, provide appropriate chews, and your Sheltie will soon learn what he's allowed to do.

If your Sheltie likes to rip things up and chew them, don't leave him unsupervised. If he has the opportunity to shred books and magazines and tear up your sofa cushions, that's your fault, not his. With maturity, most Shelties can be trusted with the run of the house, but until you know that your dog is reliable, confine him to his crate with a nice Nylabone chew toy or natural bone to play

How to Relieve Teething Discomfort

Puppies begin to replace their baby (deciduous) teeth with permanent teeth at around four months of age. You can make your pup more comfortable while he's teething by giving him:

- Nylabone chew toys
- a raw carrot
- plain ice cubes, or "soupsicles," made of low-sodium chicken, beef, or vegetable broth frozen into ice cubes

with when you can't watch him, and keep him in the room with you when you're available to do so. That makes much more sense than putting your belongings or your dog's—not to mention your temper—at risk by granting too much freedom prematurely.

Jumping Up

Even though Shelties are not big animals, you don't want your dog to jump on you or other people. A dog who jumps up can make a mess of your clothes, scratch your exposed skin, and even knock down or injure a child or frail adult. It's important to realize, though, that your dog's goal in jumping up is not to wreck your clothes or hurt you. He jumps up mostly because he likes you and wants your attention. (How often have you seen a dog jump up on someone he doesn't like?) And in fairness, you and other people have probably rewarded him for jumping up. Remember, you're training your dog all the time, and so are your family and friends. When he jumps up and you pet him or pick him up, you are rewarding him. When you get excited and push him away, he's delighted that you want to play.

Solution

To teach your Sheltie not to jump up, you must be consistent in your response. You also need to try to get other people to cooperate when they interact with your dog (which is usually more challenging). If your Sheltie is a puppy, teach him from the day you bring him home that jumping up doesn't get the results he wants, and you'll never have a problem. If you adopt an older Sheltie, or you already have one who has not been taught to stay down, the lesson may take a little longer to sink in. With consistency, though, he will learn.

One way to train your Sheltie not to jump up is to completely ignore him when he does. To make this method work, you must be patient and plan ahead. For instance, don't interact with your dog when you're wearing clothes that aren't dog safe; clothes that are washable and no great loss if they get torn are good training choices. If you have to, get up earlier, take care of your dog, and then confine him before you get dressed for work. When you get home, change your clothes before you greet your dog. This is particularly important because he'll be excited to see you if you've been gone a while.

When you do interact with your dog, pet him as long as he keeps his feet on the floor. If he jumps up, fold your arms over your chest, turn your back, look up or away, and be quiet. If he's used to getting your attention by jumping up, he'll no doubt keep trying for a bit. Eventually, though, he'll realize that you morph into a very boring human when he behaves inappropriately. When he stops jumping up, talk to him calmly and pet him. If he jumps up again, go into nonresponsive mode. When he figures out that jumping on you gets him the opposite of what he wants, he'll stop doing it. With puppies, this method usually works fairly quickly (but you have to harden your heart because puppies are so cute!). If you're retraining an older dog, it may take a bit longer, but continued training will pay off. As with all training, you need to be absolutely consistent. If you ignore your dog for jumping part of the time, but reward him by talking to him (loudly, no doubt!), pushing him off of you, or getting excited at other times, he'll keep trying to get you to play his game.

Another way to train your Sheltie not to jump up requires that you give him some additional obedience training (which you should anyway). When you think he's about to jump on you or someone else, give him a command; *sit* or *down* work well. Don't forget to praise him and occasionally reward him for obeying. Although this method works well for some people and dogs, it has two big potential pitfalls. Obviously, your Sheltie must understand the command you give every time, so it must be a special word used just for this particular behavior. And again, you must calmly give the command only once. Yelling "Sit, sit, sit!" as your dog leaps up on Aunt Susie will confuse him and won't teach your dog anything except that you are excitable. And that's the second problem

Dogs jump up because they are seeking attention. One way to train your Sheltie not to jump up is to completely ignore him when he does so, not by rewarding him with treats or petting.

with the method. Your smart little Sheltie may learn that he can get you worked up by jumping—what fun, he thinks! So make sure that you remain calm, assertive, and that you have control (use a leash if necessary) whenever you use this method.

Whatever method you use to teach your Sheltie not to jump up, there are some things you should avoid. Your Sheltie jumps up to seek attention, and if you push him down while petting him, or pet him while he's still on you, you're giving him exactly what he wants. Wait until he gets off, or use a leash to pull him gently off, and have him sit before giving him attention. Never knee, kick, or hit your dog for jumping up. You could seriously injure him, and you will certainly teach him not to trust you. It's much more effective and fair to calmly and patiently teach him that polite behavior gets him what he wants and jumping up does not.

Mouthing and Biting

Like all dogs, Shelties use their teeth when playing with other dogs but also in their own defense whenever necessary. If your Sheltie is a puppy, he needs to learn from his first day home that canine teeth do not belong on human skin, even in play.

But why do puppies mouth and nibble us in the first place? Dogs use their mouths to explore their world much in the same way we use our hands. They play with each other by grabbing, licking, and pulling with their mouths. Although a puppy with a normal temperament won't mean to hurt you, his teeth are sharp enough to break human skin. So you must teach your puppy not to mouth and bite.

Solution

One way to teach your puppy not to mouth and bite is by

making those behaviors counterproductive. If your puppy mouths you, get up, walk away, and ignore him for a minute or so. Then go back to playing with him; throw a toy, gently rub his tummy, or just pet him. Anything that does not encourage him to mouth or bite you. If he does, get up and ignore him again. If he pulls on your clothes or bites your ankles, leave the room for a minute and ignore him. Then come back and resume play. Most puppies catch on very quickly.

Another method is to redirect your puppy's mouthing away from your tender skin to a toy or chew toy that he is allowed to mouth. Give him the toy and continue to pet him. If he insists on mouthing and biting you instead of the toy, use the walk-away method outlined earlier. Before long, your Sheltie will understand that hands are wonderful belly rubbers and ear scratchers, but are off limits for gnawing.

If your puppy is more persistent than most, leave him completely alone for a minute or so, taking the toys with you if necessary. Put him in his crate or a confined area to keep him out of trouble, but do it calmly and quietly so that he won't associate the crate with punishment, just "time out." When he's calm and quiet, come back, let him out, and resume play. You have to be consistent, but if nipping always makes his playmates leave, he'll soon quit.

Keep in mind, too, that puppies and adolescents sometimes get cranky when they're tired, just like young children. If your young Sheltie has been playing for a while and gets hyperactive and mouthy, he may just need a nap. Calmly put him in his crate with a chew toy. He'll probably whine "I don't wanna go to bed!" for a minute or two, then fall sound asleep.

Whatever you do, *never* hit your Sheltie for mouthing or nipping (or anything else, for that matter). Hitting nearly always causes more problems than you had to start with and is never an appropriate way to interact with an animal.

Those sharp puppy teeth are annoying and potentially painful, but mouthing is normal puppy behavior. A lot of puppy play sounds aggressive—puppies growl and snarl and bark at each other, but it is play, the puppy version of cops and robbers, with growls instead of "Bang, Bang!" Aggression—serious growling, guarding, and biting meant to inflict real harm—is something else entirely.

Resource Guarding

Resource guarding, a specific type of aggressive behavior, is a common problem in dogs who have not been taught that it's unacceptable. A resource is anything the dog believes to have value: food, a toy, a dog bed, your bed or favorite chair, even a particular person. Although those "funniest video" television shows treat snarling dogs hunkered over toys as a joke, there's nothing funny about unchecked guarding behavior. Teach your Sheltie that guarding is unacceptable. He must always remember that everything he has, he has by your good graces, and as his alpha pack leader, you can take whatever you want from him at any time, not by force or aggression, but because he respects your rights as his superior.

Solution

Teach your Sheltie that you control the good things in his life, not by bullying him, but through basic obedience training and consistency. Have him work for you (sit, lie down, stay, whatever) to earn play, toys, or food. If he challenges you for control of anything, don't yell, threaten, or hit him. Simply take away his

Teach your Sheltie that guarding is unacceptable. You should be able to take whatever you want from him at any time.

Changing Old Habits

If you've adopted an adult Shetland Sheepdog, or if you've allowed your dog to form some bad habits, don't despair because most problems can be fixed—regardless of your dog's age! Here are some necessary steps to take, and the sooner the better:

- Be sure your Sheltie gets plenty of exercise. Many problem behaviors are related to boredom.

- Be sure the source of the problem behavior isn't health-related. Schedule a checkup and tell your vet everything you can about unusual or sudden changes in your dog's behavior, such as when the behavior started, how long it's been going on, when the behavior occurs, anything that you think may be triggering the behavior, etc.

- Take your dog through a good basic obedience class. Many problem behaviors clear up when the dog is offered more structure and kind but firm rules for good behavior.

- Prevent your Sheltie from behaving badly. For instance, if he's naughty when you're not there, crate him when you can't supervise him.

- Break the pattern that promotes the problem behavior, and replace the old habit with an acceptable new habit.

privileges. Make the toy he thinks he owns disappear (all his toys if necessary). Dole out his dinner a few morsels at a time, having him obey a command (*sit, lie down*) for each mouthful. Make him stay off the furniture until he acknowledges your authority. Continue working on basic obedience skills. Most Shelties are naturally submissive to people and readily accept their subordinate status. If your dog is guarding resources from your other dogs and they are squabbling with one another, assert your power as their pack leader and remove whatever they're arguing about.

Nipping resource guarding in the bud is by far the best approach. If your Sheltie has already developed a pattern of aggressive guarding, be careful and get help immediately from a qualified trainer or behaviorist.

Most behavioral problems occur because the dog doesn't understand the household rules. It's your job to teach your Sheltie what's expected and allowed. If you're as smart, patient, and forgiving as a Shetland Sheepdog, you and your dog can learn together, avoid or overcome most problems, and become even better friends in the process.

ADVANCED TRAINING AND ACTIVITIES

With Your Shetland Sheepdog

The Shetland Sheepdog is nothing if not versatile. Many Shelties compete successfully in a variety of sports and take part in noncompetitive activities as well. Training your Sheltie and participating with him in one or more activities will not only be fun, but will help strengthen the bond between you and your dog. It will also help channel his physical and mental energy into "legal" pursuits and reinforce the basic obedience training we've already discussed, making him a happier, more pleasant companion.

The sports and activities introduced in this chapter are just a sampling of the many ways you and your Sheltie can spend time together. To learn more, consult your local Shetland Sheepdog or training club, as well as training books, magazines, and the Internet. You and your dog can snuggle up to watch *Animal Planet* later. For now, get out there and have some fun!

FUN AND FITNESS: NONCOMPETITIVE ACTIVITIES

There are plenty of organized sports that you and your Sheltie can explore, but some of the best times to be had with him are the simplest: a walk or jog through the neighborhood, a ramble through the woods, or a backpacking trip together. Let's look at a few, and how you can keep them safe and pleasurable.

Going on Foot

Shetland Sheepdogs make outstanding walking, jogging, or running buddies. Although these simple activities require little in the way of equipment or planning, they will help keep both of you in shape. Pedestrian activities do pose a few very real dangers, though. A few precautions will keep you and your dog safer and make your experiences more enjoyable.

If either you or your dog is just beginning an exercise program, start slowly with 15- to 20-minute walks at a comfortable speed. Keep in mind that any activity is better than no activity. Increase the length, speed, and difficulty of your walks over time if you like, but

Whether you are participating in noncompetitive activities or organized sports, working regularly with your Sheltie will strengthen the bond between you, direct his energy in a positive way, and help keep him fit and trim.

don't push yourselves to the point of injury. Where's the fun in that?

If you haven't had checkups in a while, a visit to your vet (and your physician) is a good idea. If your Sheltie is overweight or out of condition, or if he's very young, elderly, or has recently recovered from an illness or injury, ask your vet to design a safe conditioning program and, possibly, a weight-loss diet. Remember, too, that although he doesn't need good walking shoes like you do, his feet do need regular attention to prevent injuries. Trim his nails, and check that his foot pads are in good condition. You may also want to trim the hair on his paws, especially between his toes, to keep them free of dirt, debris, and moisture.

When in public places, keep your Sheltie on leash. Most cities and parks, and many other jurisdictions, require dogs to be on leash to keep them from bothering other people and animals and to prevent them from entering restricted areas. Aside from the legal requirements, though, a leash assures that you know where your dog is at all times, keeps him from getting lost, and may save his life. No matter how reliable you think your dog is, one quick lapse to chase a squirrel or a car could end in tragedy. Besides, not everyone likes dogs or appreciates having them approach, and the

Safety First

Be sensible about how you exercise your Sheltie. Whatever activity or sport you choose, start out slowly and don't try to progress too quickly. Be sure your dog is in condition for whatever you ask him to do, and warm him up before each performance. Be especially cautious with puppies and adolescents whose bones and joints are susceptible to permanent injury. Whatever your dog's age, don't ask him to do things for which he lacks proper training. And remember that people, too, can be injured when playing with dogs. To keep your Sheltie and the people who love him safe, follow these guidelines:

- Attach an identification tag to your dog's collar, and have your vet insert a microchip for permanent identification in case your dog becomes lost.

- If you walk or jog at twilight or after dark, wear light-colored or reflective clothing and have your dog wear a reflective collar or vest.

- No matter how well trained you believe your Sheltie to be, don't let him off leash outdoors except in safely fenced areas, and keep him on leash when he's not inside a fence. One lapse in training could get him killed. Besides, in most places a leash is required by law.

- Don't run your dog alongside a bicycle wearing a regular leash or off leash. He could pull you over or run into the bike. If you want to ride with your dog beside you, special devices are available that safely attach a dog to a bicycle. You can find them through pet supply stores or online.

- Don't run your dog alongside your vehicle. Your Sheltie's herding instinct makes him prone to chasing vehicles, and it's a life-threatening impulse that you should curb, not encourage. Besides, one small error in judgment on your part or his could get him killed or maimed.

- Running on hard pavement or gravel can cause injuries to your Sheltie's feet, bones, and joints, so try to keep him on grass, dirt, or other softer surfaces.

- Be alert to chemicals in your dog's environment, and do what you can to limit his exposure to them. Lawn and garden chemicals can enter your Sheltie's body through his feet, skin, respiratory system, and digestive system and can make him very ill, as can salt and other ice-melting chemicals that stick to his feet in winter. If he likes to swim, he may be exposed to chlorine, petroleum products, lawn chemicals, pesticides, and other potentially hazardous substances, as well as certain parasites. Household chemicals, including some cleaning products, can also cause acute and chronic health problems.

- Check your Sheltie frequently for lumps, bumps, cuts, and other exercise-related injuries, especially on his feet, legs, ears, and eyes.

- If your dog shows signs of overexertion (very heavy panting, irregular breathing, stumbling, and reluctance to go on), slow down or stop and rest.

- Don't exercise your dog strenuously right before or right after he eats, and learn to recognize signs of bloat.

- Avoid strenuous activity during hot weather, especially when humidity is high, and offer your dog cool water every 20 to 30 minutes. Go out early in the morning or in the evening, or keep outings short. Keep him in the shade as much as possible to keep him cooler and to prevent sunburn (yes, dogs get sunburn). Avoid hot surfaces like concrete, blacktop, brick, or tile—they can burn your dog's foot pads, and they reflect heat, which can raise your dog's body temperature to life-threatening levels. Monitor your dog for signs of heat exhaustion or heat stroke, which can cause permanent brain and organ damage, or death, in a matter of minutes.

- Never leave your dog in a vehicle in warm weather, even with the windows open.

- Don't allow young children to walk your dog without adult supervision, and use outings as a chance to reinforce safety rules. Allow more freedom to older children on an individual basis, and monitor their dog-walking skills from time to time. Also, to avoid serious injuries, teach children never to slide their hands through the loop of a leash or to put a leash around any part of their bodies, particularly their necks. (The same goes for adults!)

last thing you want is for your Sheltie to run up to an aggressive dog.

Make sure that your dog's collar fits properly. Check frequently to be sure that your collar and leash are both in good repair; when you're a mile from home on foot, broken equipment is no fun and can put your dog at risk of injury or worse.

Good leash manners are essential for safe dog walking. Shelties, like many herding dogs, are prone to circling and darting back and forth on walks, and although that's an entertaining behavior at times, it can also be dangerous. Your dog needs to learn to walk calmly on one side of the person with the leash; the left side is conventional for dog sports, but if you don't plan to show your dog and prefer that he be on your right, that's fine. If your Sheltie's leash manners leave something to be desired, take him through a good obedience class.

Even if your dog has good leash manners, whoever walks him needs to be able to control him under all circumstances. Children often want to walk dogs, and the Sheltie's size makes him more suitable for small people than many larger breeds. But even a Sheltie can put a lot of power into pulling, and a child who can't control a dog under all circumstances could be seriously injured. Nor is your Sheltie's behavior the only concern. Things happen on walks that are hard even for adults to manage—encounters with stray dogs, for instance, or situations that require judgment that a child may lack. Young children should never walk a dog without a responsible adult along to supervise. An older child may be capable, but should be taught safety rules and monitored from time to time.

Hiking and Backpacking

Shetland Sheepdogs are natural companions for nature walks; they have the stamina for a hike, and the interest and senses to notice things we might overlook. Your Sheltie can learn to wear a lightweight backpack to carry his own food and water (build him up slowly to carrying weight). He can also do his environmental duty by carrying his scooped and bagged feces out of the wilderness in his backpack for proper disposal.

Whether you and your dog are going for an afternoon hike or a week-long adventure, a little planning will make the experience more enjoyable. Here are some things you can do to keep your dog safe and healthy and make your adventure more fun:

- Be sure that dogs are permitted where you want to hike—many state and national parks, wildlife refuges, and other sites do not allow dogs. If dogs are permitted, do your part to keep it that way by following the rules. Your dog should be under control at all times. Even if leashes are not required (they are required in most places), a leash will keep your Sheltie safer and ensure that he doesn't disturb people, other pets, or wildlife.

- Ask your veterinarian if she recommends any special vaccinations or precautions against bacterial and viral diseases that your dog might encounter in natural areas that he wouldn't in your neighborhood.

- In warm weather, ask your vet to recommend an effective tick repellant and killer, and be sure your Sheltie is protected against heartworm disease (see Chapter 8).

- Grooming is just as important in the great outdoors as in the show ring. Before you head out, trim your Sheltie's nails, and smooth any rough edges that could catch and tear. Check his feet for cuts, thorns, or other problems before, every so often during, and after every hike. When you finish a hike, remove burrs and other debris from his coat.

- Get your dog (and yourself!) in shape with shorter hikes before tackling a long one.

Although you don't need a lot of special equipment for most outings, a few items will be useful. Your leash will probably get dirty and wet, so waterproof your leather leash or use a washable nylon or cotton leash for hiking. Retractable leashes are good in some situations, but they tend to wrap around trees and brush, and many parks require that leashes be 6 feet (2 m) in length or shorter. Carry a spare collar and leash in your Sheltie's backpack or your own—they won't do you any good back in the car or tent. A few lightweight first-aid supplies, such as tweezers in case your dog picks up a thorn or tick, antiseptic cleansing towels, and a topical antibiotic, are also a good idea.

Carry clean water, and bring a bowl or teach your dog to drink from a squirt bottle. Easy-to-carry collapsible bowls are available from pet supply stores. Offer your dog water at regular intervals to prevent dehydration and overheating, and try not to let him drink from water sources along the way because they are often contaminated with bacteria, parasites, and chemicals.

In hot weather, be alert to signs that your Sheltie is overheating. If you hike at higher altitudes than your normal environment, allow extra time for breaks, and offer your dog water at frequent intervals. Proper hydration helps fend off altitude sickness.

Practicing good trail etiquette will help ensure that dogs remain welcome in at least some parks and similar areas. Teach your Sheltie to sit or lie quietly beside the trail to let other hikers pass, and discourage barking. Tell a reliable friend where you're going and how long you'll be gone, and check in when you get back, especially if you are hiking alone with your dog.

GOOD DOGS, GOOD WORKS

Many Shelties contribute to the happiness of people beyond their own households. Some, with the help of their owners, demonstrate the benefits of basic obedience training and the confidence and manners it fosters. Others take those basics a step further, bringing comfort to people who need it.

The AKC Canine Good Citizen® Program

The Canine Good Citizen® (CGC) program was developed by the American Kennel Club (AKC) to promote basic training and responsible dog care. To become an official Canine Good Citizen, your Sheltie must pass the CGC test, which includes the following ten subtests that simulate some of the conditions you might encounter when out in the community with your dog:

Test 1: A "friendly stranger" will approach, shake your hand, and speak to you, as might happen on a walk. You dog must remain quietly beside you without acting shy or resentful.

Test 2: The friendly stranger will pet your dog's head and body. Once again, your dog must not act shy or resentful.

Test 3: Your dog must be clean and well groomed and appear to be well cared for, and he must allow one of the testers to comb or brush his coat and gently check his ears and front feet.

Test 4: Your dog must walk calmly beside you on leash while making several turns and stopping with you at least twice.

Test 5: Your dog must walk with you past and among at least three strangers, showing that he is polite and under

The Canine Good Citizen program encourages owners to foster and encourage good manners in their dogs.

control in public.

Test 6: Your dog must demonstrate some basic training by sitting, lying down, and staying on command.

Test 7: Your dog must stay where you tell him and then come when you call him from 10 feet (3 m) away. (A long line will remain fastened to his collar for safety.)

Test 8: Your dog must walk with you to approach and meet another person with a dog and must show no more than casual interest in the other dog.

Test 9: Your dog must stay calm when faced with two distractions that you could realistically encounter in your community (for instance, a falling object, a person in a wheelchair or walker, or a jogger or bicyclist passing by).

Test 10: Your dog must stay calm and polite when left with one of the testers while you go out of sight for three minutes.

CGC evaluators will consider your dog's response to people, strange dogs, loud noises, and visual distractions. Your Sheltie will also need to walk politely on leash and respond to basic obedience commands (*sit, lie down, stay*, and *come*). He must be reasonably clean, well groomed, and vaccinated against rabies as required by law. To pass the CGC test and earn the CGC designation, your dog must pass all ten subtests.

During the test, your dog will remain on leash at all times, and

Therapy Dogs Versus Service Dogs

Although therapy dogs and service dogs both work hard to make life better for people, they are not the same thing. Service dogs are working dogs who undergo aptitude testing and intensive specialized training to learn the skills necessary to assist people as guide dogs for the blind, hearing dogs for the deaf, general assistance dogs, medical alert dogs, and so on. The Americans with Disabilities Act (ADA) gives service dogs full legal access to virtually every place their owners can go.

Most therapy dogs are full-time pets and part-time volunteers who visit hospitals, nursing homes, hospices, schools, libraries, and other facilities. Therapy dogs must be friendly, well-behaved, and mentally stable, and should have at least some obedience training. Ideally, they have been tested and certified by one of the therapy organizations, but therapy dogs do not have to undergo specialized training, and they have no special legal rights. They do, however, profoundly affect the people they touch physically and emotionally.

he must wear a properly fitted buckle or slip (choke) collar made of leather, fabric, or chain. No other types of collars, harnesses, or head halters are allowed. You will need to bring your dog's brush or comb for the grooming and handling subtest. Most clubs charge a nominal fee for the test, and if your dog passes, you have the option of paying an additional small fee to the AKC for an official certificate and collar tag.

The CGC test evaluates your dog's "good citizenship," so in addition to performing the subtests, he is required to behave as you'd expect a good citizen to behave. If he growls, snaps, bites, attacks or tries to attack another dog or a person at any time, whether before, during, or after the test, you will be required to remove him from the test area, and he will not be awarded the CGC certification.

If your aspiring good citizen doesn't pass the test, don't be embarrassed or discouraged. The CGC test is not only a chance to earn a certificate, but also an opportunity to find out what behaviors your dog still needs to work on to make him reliable outside a training environment. Keep in mind that the testing environment—like the real world—is filled with new sights and sounds, new people and dogs, and if you're a little anxious about the test (as many people are), your Sheltie will pick up on your feelings and become anxious, too. If he doesn't pass the test, keep training, love your dog, and try again later.

Animal-Assisted Service and Therapy Work

If you like to volunteer and can commit to a regular schedule, and if your dog is obedient, well behaved, and you both enjoy meeting people, you and your Sheltie might want to join the ranks of therapy dog teams who bring joy to people in a variety of environments. To be successful, your dog must like people and be comfortable in new situations, and he must have enough obedience training to be reliable.

The term "therapy dog" is a sort of catch-all term used to refer to a dog who works, usually as a volunteer with his owner, in two different types of settings. If he works in animal-assisted activities (AAA), your dog will visit people in any of a variety of locations, including nursing homes, hospitals, hospices, shelters, schools, libraries, and so on. Dogs trained for AAA have even been brought to disaster sites, including the World Trade Center, to comfort victims and emergency workers. Although these visits are proven to be highly beneficial for recipients, they are not technically considered to be "therapy" because no professional therapist is involved, and the dog's impact on people is not formally evaluated. In animal-assisted therapy (AAT), on the other hand, a professional therapist, teacher, or doctor directs the dog's activities and evaluates the benefits in concrete terms.

Although some institutions will allow you to bring your dog for visits with no formal credentials, there are good reasons to have him evaluated by one of the organizations that certify therapy dogs. For one thing, the evaluation process provides impartial verification that your dog has the temperament and behavior necessary for therapy work. These national organizations also provide insurance coverage for their members, which is an important consideration. Some local organizations also certify therapy dogs, but the value of such certification is highly variable, so check the credentials of the personnel and the benefits to you and your dog before you join. Many hospitals, nursing homes, libraries, and other institutions, as well as training and kennel clubs, have therapy programs, if you prefer to work within a group.

Volunteering With Your Dog

You can learn more about animal-assisted service and therapy work from the following organizations:

Delta Society
(425) 226-7357
www.deltasociety.org

Therapy Dogs Incorporated
(877) 843-7364
www.therapydogs.com

Therapy Dogs International
(973) 252-9800
www.tdi-dog.org

BEAUTY IS AS BEAUTY DOES: PERFORMANCE SPORTS FOR SHETLAND SHEEPDOGS

Shetland Sheepdogs excel at many activities, and they are always in the top rankings in competitive obedience, rally, agility, flyball, and some other sports. If you enjoy setting and pursuing goals, and you like to spend time training your dog and fraternizing with like-minded dog lovers, you may want to get involved with one or more canine sports. Trust me, most Shelties revel in the chance to use their bodies and their brains in human-approved pursuits, and the training you do will strengthen the bond between you and your dog. You can participate just for fun, to earn titles, or to become highly competitive—anything's possible with a Sheltie.

Runnin' and Jumpin': Agility and Flyball

Agility, one of the fastest growing sports in the world, requires the dog to negotiate a course of jumps, tunnels, and other obstacles in the proper order and within a specified time limit. Shelties, with their natural athleticism and eagerness to please, excel at the sport, and dominate the rankings in their height divisions.

You can practice many agility skills with simple homemade equipment, running off some of that herding-dog energy and having lots of fun with your dog. If you catch the agility bug—beware, many Sheltie owners do—your Sheltie can compete and earn titles through several organizations that sanction agility competition at all levels, from novice through advanced.

In flyball, dogs run relay races in teams of four. Each team member races down a lane over a series of four hurdles and hits a peddle on a spring-loaded box. A tennis ball is released, and the dog grabs the ball and races back to the starting line. Again, their speed, athleticism, and biddability make Shelties good at the flyball game. Oh, and a bonus for most Shelties: There's lots of barking in flyball!

With their natural athleticism, Shetland Sheepdogs excel at many activities, and they are always in the top rankings in competitive obedience, agility, flyball, and rally, as well as in other sports.

Teamwork Is Everything: Obedience and Rally

Another sport at which Shelties excel is competitive obedience, which is meant to demonstrate the dog's mastery of exercises that simulate useful real-life tasks. Although the dog's performance of the test exercises is usually stressed, the handler must also follow certain rules, and the teamwork between dog and handler also factors into the final score.

A number of organizations throughout the world offer obedience titling programs in which Shelties compete with great success. (See Resources.) The rules vary somewhat from one organization to another, so before you enter a trial, be sure to obtain and read the pertinent rule book. Smart as he is, that's one thing your Shetland Sheepdog can't do for you!

Rally, or rally obedience, is one of the newest titling sports for dogs. Begun less than a decade ago, rally trials have become extremely popular. More informal and less rigid and demanding than competitive obedience or agility, rally requires the dog-and-handler team to demonstrate specific skills as they negotiate a predetermined course of stations. Rally is an excellent sport for novice dogs and handlers, and for dogs who cannot perform in agility or advanced obedience due to age or physical limitation.

Many obedience competitors also participate in rally trials as a fun alternative to the more formal obedience rings.

The Association of Pet Dog Trainers (APDT) and the AKC both sanction rally trials, and the United Kennel Club (UKC), Australian Shepherd Club of America (ASCA), and other organizations are reportedly developing rally programs as well.

Tracking

In the sport of tracking, your dog follows a specific scent trail. The fact is, your Sheltie already knows how to track—just watch him follow bunny trails through the back yard! In fact, even very young puppies have terrific olfactory abilities. Because tracking doesn't put stress on young bones and joints (see "Safety First"), it's a good activity for using up some puppy energy and building trust and teamwork between you and your dog. Your job as a tracking handler is to teach your dog which track you want him to follow and to learn to trust him while he works. Besides, watching your dog follow a trail by scent, which we can't see but can only imagine, is great fun.

Informal tracking sessions don't need to be time consuming, but preparing for a tracking test requires a considerable investment of time. You also need access to reasonably large and varied pieces of land, and both dog and handler

What If Your Sheltie Isn't Registered?

If your Sheltie is not registered, don't worry—you can still participate in organized dog sports (except for conformation). Here's how:

- The American Kennel Club (AKC) offers the Individual Limited Privileges (ILP) number for dogs who appear to be purebred and who are spayed or neutered. The ILP entitles your dog to enter AKC performance events and to earn titles and other honors in obedience, rally, agility, tracking, and herding.

- The United Kennel Club (UKC) offers individual registration that will entitle your Sheltie to participate in UKC events.

- The Australian Shepherd Club of America (ASCA) welcomes all dogs in its performance events, including obedience, agility, tracking, and stockdog trials. To earn titles, your Sheltie will need an ASCA Tracking Number. Applications are available from ASCA. Other specialized organizations, including the North American Dog Agility Council (NADAC) and the United States Dog Agility Association (USDAA) for agility, and the American Herding Breed Association (AHBA) for herding, also welcome Shelties.

must be fit enough to walk long distances over rough terrain. Many obedience clubs have tracking groups that train together, and tracking clubs also exist in some locales. If you like to earn titles with your Sheltie, the AKC and ASCA both offer titling programs, as do other organizations throughout the world.

Herding and Stockdog Events

There's nothing quite like the thrill of seeing a dog's instinct kick in as he engages in the activity he was bred for—and as their name attests, for Shetland Sheepdogs that activity is herding animals, especially sheep. Not all Shelties have what it takes to work livestock day to day, or to compete successfully in herding trials, but most Shelties do have some inclination to gather animals and move them around.

The AKC, ASCA, American Herding Breed Association (AHBA), and other organizations offer herding tests and trials in which Shelties can earn titles. If you'd like to try herding for fun or for competition, your local Sheltie club can direct you to clinics and instructors in your area, and to instinct tests. Although the rules and procedures vary among the organizations, typically a "test" for a title is a noncompetitive titling event in which dogs are required to perform certain tasks, and they either pass or do not pass. For example, to earn the Herding Tested (HT) title, your dog must move several sheep across a small arena, stop on command, and come when called. Higher-level tests and trial classes require more training. If you want to take herding lessons with your Sheltie, experienced handlers recommend that you find an instructor who has worked with Shelties or with herding breeds that have a similar style of working close to the livestock.

Flying Disc

Ever throw a flying disc for your Sheltie to catch or chase? If you and your dog really enjoy that game, you may find organized canine disc sports to your liking.

The International Disc Dog Handlers' Association (IDDHA) sanctions canine disc events throughout the world, including a test program and a titling program. To compete for titles, you and your dog must first demonstrate basic teamwork by successfully completing the IDDHA test program. Then you may enter competitive events and earn titles, including the BDD

(Basic Disc Dog), ADD (Advanced Disc Dog), MDD (Master Disc Dog), CSF (Combined Skills Freestyle title), and DDX (Disc Dog Expert).

Skyhoundz, a separate organization, offers competition in two divisions: Sport and Open. In Open, teams compete for invitations to the World Championships.

Dancing With Dogs

You may have seen video clips on the Internet of stirring dance routines performed by human–canine teams. These teams are participating in canine musical freestyle, a competitive sport that combines obedience training, dance moves, and music to demonstrate teamwork and rapport between dog and handler. Routines are set to music, and the handler interprets the music with body, arm, and leg motions while the dog performs various movements. Essentially, they dance together. The handlers and many of the dogs wear costumes, and some turn their dances into dramatic skits. In competition, both the handler and the dog are judged, and although all components of the performance affect the score, judges emphasize teamwork.

The World Canine Freestyle Organization (WCFO) and Musical Canine Sports International (MCSI) both offer titles at several levels, as well as classes for more than one dog, or more than one dog-and-handler team.

Conformation Shows

You've probably watched Westminster, Crufts, and other dog shows on television, and perhaps you've been to local dog shows in person. Those events in which the dogs are trotted around the ring and lined up for judging are called conformation shows. The traditional purpose of the conformation show was to evaluate the quality of potential breeding stock. Although the dogs in the ring on any particular day are competing against one another, each dog is also supposed to be judged against the breed standard to see how well he conforms to that measure of excellence (see Chapter 1). However, because such shows began as a means to judge breeding stock, most show-sponsoring organizations still limit competition to intact (not spayed or neutered) dogs.

How Conformation Shows Work

In the United States, several organizations offer conformation shows and championships. Each is set up a little differently, and the requirements for a championship vary. Because the AKC conformation program is the best known and largest, and it has served as a model for some of the others, I'll explain how the AKC system works. If you want to show your Sheltie in a different organization, check their rules before you enter.

At the Westminster show—probably the best-known dog show to most Americans—all the dogs are already champions, so competition begins with Best of Breed classes in each breed. At most other shows a majority of the dogs entered have not yet "finished," that is, earned their championships, so judging begins with classes organized according to age (6 to 9 Months, 9 to 12 Months, 12 to 18 Months), breeding (Bred by Exhibitor, American Bred), and sometimes color or other factors. Dogs (males) are judged initially against dogs, and bitches (females) against bitches, and in each class the dogs are ranked from first to fourth place. The first-place winners from all the classes for each sex then compete against one another, and the individuals who win at this level are the Winners' Dog (WD) and Winners' Bitch (WB). They are the only two animals who earn points toward their championships.

At the next level of competition, the Winners' Dog and Winners' Bitch compete against specials (dogs and bitches who have already earned their championships), and the judge chooses one individual as Best of Breed (BOB). She then chooses the Best of Opposite Sex (BOS), a rather confusing term that simply means the best individual of the opposite sex to the BOB. If the Best of Breed is a dog (male), the Best of Opposite Sex is a bitch (female), and vice versa. The judge also chooses between the Winners' Dog and Winners' Bitch for the Best of Winners (BOW). It is possible for the WD or WB to win Best of Breed, in which case he or she is automatically Best of Winners. Finally, the WD or WB may win Best of Opposite Sex, making him or her Best of Winners unless the other "Winner" won Best of Breed. Although it seems confusing at first, it's really quite logical once you know the terms.

At Shetland Sheepdog specialty shows, Best of Breed is the highest award possible in conformation because only one breed is present. Most shows, though, are "all-breed" shows, so the pyramid rises even higher. If your Sheltie wins Best of Breed, he will then compete at the group level against the Best of Breed winners from all the other Herding Group breeds represented at the show. But how, you ask, can a Shetland Sheepdog be judged against, say, a Bouvier des Flandres, or a Pembroke Welsh Corgi, when the breeds are so different from one another? The simple answer is that your Sheltie is judged not against the other dogs, but against the Shetland Sheepdog breed standard. In other words, the judge is looking for the animal who best represents the standard for his or her own breed. But there's more to winning the group than just being "correct" according to the standard. This is where the "show" part of dog show really comes into play, because the overall quality of the dogs tends to be very good at this level. To win the group, the dog must have that extra intangible presence that makes the judge take notice—or in dog show lingo, the dog must "ask for the win." The judges choose what they consider to be the best four animals in each of the seven breed groups. Those seven dogs then compete for the high honor of Best in Show (BIS).

How Championships Are Earned

Once again, I will use the AKC system as an example because it is the most prevalent organization in the United States. Other organizations award championships a bit differently, so check the rules for the group that interests you. In all cases, your dog must be registered with the organization that sanctions the show before you can enter.

To become an AKC Champion (CH) (sometimes called a "breed champion"), your Sheltie must earn 15 points under three different judges, including two majors (a win of 3, 4, or 5 points) under two different judges. The number of points your dog earns at any given show is determined by the number of dogs he or she defeats. The AKC publishes schedules that show how many entries are needed for how many points in different regions of the country, so be sure to consult an up-to-date

During conformation shows, dogs are judged against the standard for the breed.

schedule of points. If your dog wins points, it's also a good idea to check with the show superintendent after the judge turns in her book to be sure the win was correctly recorded. Mistakes don't happen often, but you still want to know that the correct entry number was recorded.

Learn to Play the Game

If your Sheltie measures up as a conformation prospect, you need to learn the ropes. The professional and experienced owners/ handlers you see on television make it seem easy, but showing a dog in conformation is harder than it looks. You may want to hire a professional handler to show your dog. If so, choose very carefully; experienced owners and breeders can guide you and tell you what to avoid. Or, you may plan to show your Sheltie yourself. If so, go to shows, watch the handlers, and note how the good ones make their dogs stand out in the ring. Take at least one handling class or clinic, preferably one taught by a professional or successful amateur handler. If you can't find a class, perhaps you can pay a professional handler or an experienced Sheltie exhibitor to give you some lessons. Remember that a dog show is a "show," and presentation is important. Ideally, dogs would be judged strictly on their own merits in light of the breed standard, but in the real world your Sheltie's grooming and performance, and your own appearance and handling skills, all affect your success in the show ring.

Grooming is an essential aspect of Sheltie presentation, and preferences among Sheltie exhibitors range from a bath and a good brushing to extreme trimming and fluffing with all sorts of coat products. Whatever approach you choose, your Sheltie's coat should be clean and tidy, his feet and ears properly trimmed, his nails nice and short, and his teeth clean. You can learn a lot about show grooming from books, magazines, and web articles, but nothing takes the place of hands-on experience. Local Sheltie clubs sometimes offer grooming clinics to demonstrate technique, and some exhibitors may be willing to teach you. If your dog's breeder is nearby, she may be your best mentor because she has a stake in your dog's success.

When you're ready to take the plunge, start with a small show or a puppy match. Despite the name, puppy matches usually have classes not only for puppies from two to six months old, but also for adult dogs who don't have major points toward their championships. Match wins don't earn points toward a championship, but you and your dog can gain experience without the expense and pressure of a real show. If no matches are available in your area, look for smaller shows where, again, the pressure will be less than at large, highly competitive events. Finally, always remember that the winners and nonwinners in any particular show reflect one person's opinion on one given day. The dog who stands at the end of the lineup today may be Best of Breed tomorrow, and vice versa. Your Sheltie loves you, win or lose. When that means less than winning a piece of ribbon, it's time to find a new hobby.

Finding Your Sheltie Show or Performance Dog

Perhaps you have a pet Sheltie, and now you think you'd like to compete with him in one or more sports. Good for you; you and your dog are both going to have some wonderful times together. And the good news is that, although dogs who achieve the highest titles, best scores, and highest honors have some special traits and training, any healthy Sheltie should be able to participate

American Kennel Club Titles

If you are shopping for a puppy (or planning your Sheltie's competition career), it's helpful to know what all those initials before and after the dogs' names mean. Here are some of the titles that Shetland Sheepdogs can earn:

Agility

NA	Novice Agility
OA	Open Agility
AX	Agility Excellent
MX	Master Agility Excellent
NAJ	Novice Jumpers with Weaves
OAJ	Open Jumpers with Weaves
AXJ	Excellent Jumpers with Weaves
MXJ	Master Excellent Jumpers with Weaves
MACH	Master Agility Champion (MACH may be followed by a number designation to indicate the number of times the dog has met the requirements of the MACH title).

Herding

HT	Herding Tested
PT	Pre-Trial Tested
HS	Herding Started
HI	Herding Intermediate
HX	Herding Excellent
HC	Herding Champion

Obedience

CD	Companion Dog
CDX	Companion Dog Excellent
UD	Utility Dog
UDX	Utility Dog Excellent
NOC	National Obedience Champion
OTCH	Obedience Trial Champion

Rally

RN	Rally Novice
RA	Rally Advanced
RE	Rally Excellent
RAE	Rally Advanced Excellent

Tracking

TD	Tracking Dog
TDX	Tracking Dog Excellent
VST	Variable Surface Tracker
CT	Champion Tracker (TD,TDX, and VST)

Versatility Titles

VCD1	Versatile Companion Dog 1: Must complete CD, NA, NAJ, TD or CD, NAP, NJP, TD
VCD2	Versatile Companion Dog 2: Must complete CDX, OA, OAJ, TD or CDX, OAP, OJP, TD
VCD3	Versatile Companion Dog 3: Must Complete UD, AX, AXJ, TDX or UD, AX, AXJ,TDX
VCD4	Versatile Companion Dog 4: Must complete UDX, MX, MXJ, VST or UDX, MXP, MJP, VST
VCCH	Versatile Companion Champion: Must complete OTCH, MACH, and CT Additional Certificate

["P" following the title indicates "Preferred," in which lower jump heights are used, usually for young, older, and beginning dogs.]

When dogs are given an adequate amount of recreation time, they are healthier, happier, and better behaved.

successfully, have fun, and earn titles in performance sports, especially at the novice level.

If you want to show in conformation shows, however, be sure your dog conforms to the breed standard. A dog can be a topnotch companion, cute as the dickens, and even an outstanding competitor in performance events, and still not be right for the conformation ring. The eyes of love don't always see clearly, so try not to let your emotions keep you from looking honestly at your dog's faults as well as his virtues. If possible, have someone who knows the breed well—a Sheltie breeder or show judge, if possible—evaluate him and review the evaluation with you. Every show dog has faults, maybe a neck that's a little too short, or head that's a little too narrow. But when an individual has a lot of faults, or a disqualifying fault, he won't be competitive. Showing him will be a waste of time and money and will not reflect well on your judgment or that of your breeder among your fellow Sheltie lovers. Enjoy your dog, gain experience in performance sports if he's up to it, and if you still want to show in conformation, buy a conformation prospect.

If you don't own a Sheltie yet and you'd like to compete in one or more sports, limit your search to breeders or rescuers who show their own dogs with reasonable success in the venues that interest you and who have a history of successful placements. A breeder or rescuer who doesn't show at all, or who shows but never wins, may not be able to help you choose the right dog. Oddly enough, some people seem to think that any pup or dog who is not a conformation ring candidate is by default a performance candidate. Not so! To succeed, performance dogs must be structurally correct, physically and mentally healthy, intelligent, and obedient—in other words, they should come close to the breed standard, although size is not a factor.

When you've narrowed your search to several breeders, contact them and explain what you hope to do with your dog. Discuss whether you should start with a puppy or with a young adult. That's a particularly important decision if your goal is to show in conformation because there is no such thing as a "show puppy." A puppy can be a show prospect, but more than a few puppies who look terrific at 8 weeks do not turn out to be good conformation prospects at 8 months. They may grow too tall or not tall enough for the show ring, their bites may go off when adult teeth come in, their testicles can fail to drop, and so on. Most of the pups who don't turn out to be show dogs are still wonderful pets and—if they have the other necessary traits—good performance dogs, but if you really want to show in conformation, buying a Sheltie who is closer to maturity makes sense. Whatever sport or activity you have in mind, buying or adopting from someone who understands what the dog needs to be successful will make it more likely that you take home the Sheltie you desire.

Enjoy Each Other

If you decide to compete with your Sheltie or participate in noncompetitive activities and training, you'll find they are wonderful ways to grow closer to your dog, have fun, get some exercise, learn new things, and spend time with like-minded people. Unfortunately, you'll also run into people who seem to have forgotten what brought them to dog sports in the first place—love for a dog. Winning is exhilarating, but not at the cost of sportsmanship and good dog owning skills. Success with dogs isn't just about winning. As a wise obedience judge once told me, "A successful trial is one that you leave with a happy dog." The real treasure to be found in dog sports is the time you and your dog spend enjoying one another's company, win or lose.

8

HEALTH

of Your Shetland Sheepdog

Your Shetland Sheepdog will live a longer, healthier life if you safeguard his health. You are his protector from danger and disease, and his first line of defense when he shows signs of illness or injury. Even if your Sheltie shows no signs of ill health, routine veterinary examinations are essential to identify problems in their early stages and increase the chances that treatment will be effective if it becomes necessary. Regular care makes good sense, too, since prevention is always far better than treatment and could likely save your dog from unnecessary pain and suffering. So, let's take a look at what you can do to keep your Sheltie healthy from puppyhood to a ripe old age.

PARTNERING WITH YOUR VETERINARIAN

One of the most important people in your Sheltie's life is your veterinarian. She is your partner in your dog's health care, providing the tools and information you need to protect him from illness and to treat sickness and injuries when they occur.

Finding the Right Veterinarian

You should feel confident about your veterinarian's knowledge and skills in medicine and in her willingness to include you in planning and implementing your Sheltie's health care program.

If you have had a dog before, chances are you have already developed a longstanding relationship with a veterinarian. Still, there are times when it becomes necessary to find a new vet—if she retires, for instance, or if you move. You also may decide to change your dog's doctor for other reasons. Here are some suggestions to help you choose the best vet for your needs and your dog's long-term health.

Recommendations from your breeder, friends, and family are a good start and useful for narrowing down your choices. On the other hand, your cousin's favorite vet may not suit you, so try to interview those individuals who seem like good candidates before your dog needs care. Most veterinarians will talk to you for a few minutes at no charge, but even if you have to pay for an office visit, it's worth it to know that your Sheltie's health—in fact, his life—will be in good hands.

*Annual veterinary checkups
are essential if you want
your dog to stay healthy.*

You don't necessarily need to be friends with your vet, but
you should feel comfortable discussing your dog's care with her.
She should listen to you and answer your questions. Above all,
she should really like dogs. You should also be confident and
comfortable with the practice in which your vet works, including
veterinary technicians, assistants, receptionists, and the other vets
who may fill in when your regular vet is unavailable.

Aside from the personnel, you may want to consider some or all
of the following factors when choosing a veterinary practice:

- Do their office hours work with your schedule?
- Do they offer emergency care outside regular hours? If not, do
  they refer you to another emergency facility?
- If it is a multivet practice, can you choose the vet you will see?
  If she's not available when your dog needs care, can you see
  someone else?
- Can you get an appointment on short notice if a serious problem
  develops?
- Do they follow up-to-date vaccination protocols?
- Do they offer or support alternative approaches to prevention
  and disease?
- Are you comfortable with their payment and billing policies?
- Do they offer any discounts that you might use (such as for

multiple pets or seniors)?

- If you need to drop your dog off and pick him up later, will you be charged a boarding fee? Will you be able to see the vet when you pick your dog up?

- Do they offer other services that you may want to use, such as boarding, training, or grooming?

- Finally, are you comfortable with the physical atmosphere of the practice? It doesn't have to be a sleek, state-of-the-art facility, but the waiting room, exam rooms, holding or boarding kennels, and operating area should be clean and in good repair. Your Sheltie deserves nothing less.

ROUTINE VETERINARY CARE

Regular veterinary care, including periodic examinations and preventive medications and vaccines, are essential for your dog's health and well-being. If your Sheltie shows no obvious signs of ill health, you may be tempted to skip routine vet visits to save money. Unfortunately for your dog and your purse, lack of regular care can allow small problems to become enormous, threatening your dog's health or life, and costing you more money in the long run.

One essential component of your dog's routine health care is regular veterinary examinations. For a healthy adult Sheltie, an

Online Canine Health Resources

The Internet offers vast resources about canine health. Unfortunately, some sites also post potentially harmful misinformation. Always consult several sources, as well as your vet, before acting on what you read, and check the credentials of the site as well. Most important, the Internet should *never* replace your veterinarian as your Sheltie's first line of defense against poor health.

Many veterinarians and vet schools offer reliable online health care information, and many breed-related websites also offer information and links. The following websites are a good place to start a general search:

- American Veterinary Medical Association (AVMA): www.avma.org
- American Holistic Veterinary Medical Association (AHVMA): www.ahvma.org
- Canine Cancer Awareness, Inc.: www.caninecancerawareness.org
- Canine Epilepsy Network: www.canine-epilepsy.net
- Cornell University College of Veterinary Medicine Information Resources: partnersah.vet.cornell.edu/pet

annual checkup is usually appropriate. Puppies under one year old, elderly dogs, and dogs with chronic conditions will need to see their vets more often.

During a routine examination, your vet will check your Sheltie's:
- teeth and gums for tartar, swelling, or inflammation
- ears for infection, injury, or other problems
- eyes for pupil response and retinal appearance
- skin and coat for parasites and other problems
- weight, temperature, respiration, and heart rate
- blood chemistry for signs of disease
- fecal sample for intestinal parasites
- blood for heartworm disease (usually recommended every year if your dog takes year-round preventive medication)

If your Sheltie is due for vaccinations or immunity titer tests, your vet will give them after the exam. She will also prescribe other medications as needed and may recommend additional tests, depending on the results of the examination.

INFECTIOUS DISEASES AND VACCINATIONS

Like all living things, your Sheltie is susceptible to a number of infectious diseases, that is, diseases that spread from one animal to another, killing some and leaving others with lifelong problems. Fortunately, vaccinations are available to prevent or limit the severity of many common canine diseases.

Most canine vaccines are injected subcutaneously (under the skin) or intramuscularly (into the muscle). A few are administered by nasal sprays. Vaccines are usually given to dogs in combination shots that protect against more than one disease. Core vaccinations protect against the most common canine diseases, including rabies, distemper, parvovirus, canine infectious hepatitis, and parainfluenza. Noncore vaccinations protect against less common diseases. All dogs should receive the core vaccinations. You and your veterinarian should decide whether or not to give your dog various noncore vaccinations based on his age, health status, potential for exposure to the disease, and vaccination history, including any reactions he has had to vaccines in the past.

Vaccination Protocols

A battery of annual vaccinations used to be considered

routine for dogs, but many people have become concerned about health and behavior problems associated with their overuse. As a result, the American Veterinary Medical Association (AVMA), most veterinary colleges, and many veterinarians and dog owners have modified their vaccination protocols, although they have not yet agreed on any single approach. Puppies definitely need to be vaccinated to stimulate their immune systems and

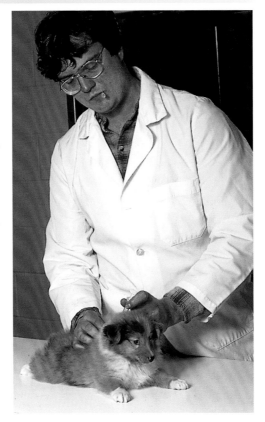

Vaccinations help protect a dog against disease.

protect them against devastating diseases. Some people believe that puppy vaccinations provide lifelong protection, while others prefer to revaccinate their dogs on rotating or multiyear schedules. Still others use titers to check the dog's antibody levels, and revaccinate only when immunity is low. The one exception is rabies, which is the only vaccination required by law in many places (see "Rabies").

Vaccination does carry some minor risk, but vaccines used properly still offer your Sheltie the best protection available against infectious diseases. Educate yourself about the benefits and risks of vaccination, and work with your veterinarian to decide which vaccines to give and on what schedule. If you're uncomfortable with one vet's approach, find another, but don't leave your Sheltie defenseless.

The following are diseases that your dog may be vaccinated against.

Coronavirus

Coronavirus is a viral disease that attacks the lining of the small intestine. Initial symptoms include depression, loss of appetite, lethargy followed by vomiting (sometimes with blood in the vomit), and projectile diarrhea that is yellowish in color and often contains blood and mucous. Because coronavirus occurs only in certain areas, many veterinarians do not recommend vaccination for dogs who are not at risk of exposure to the disease.

Distemper

Canine distemper is caused by a virus that attacks the nervous system, resulting in respiratory problems, vomiting, and diarrhea. It is highly contagious, and most puppies and about half of adult dogs who contract the disease die from it, so vaccination is essential. Dogs who do survive often lose some or all of their vision, hearing, and sense of smell, and may be partially or completely paralyzed.

Puppies normally receive a series of three or four vaccinations against distemper, and many vets recommend vaccination for adult dogs, especially in their later years.

Infectious Canine Hepatitis

Infectious canine hepatitis is caused by a virus that attacks many tissues, although it usually does the most damage to the liver. The virus is shed in the urine of infected dogs, and it is highly contagious.

Puppies are normally given a series of three shots; adult dogs may be revaccinated annually or less frequently.

Kennel Cough: Bordetella

Bordetella, also known as kennel cough, is a bacterial disease of the respiratory tract. Like the common cold in people, bordetella usually isn't very serious in an otherwise healthy adult dog, although it does cause a horrible sounding cough sometimes accompanied by copious nasal discharge. In a puppy or elderly dog, or one with other health issues, bordetella can be deadly.

There is considerable controversy about the need for and effectiveness of bordetella vaccinations for most dogs, so talk to your vet about your Sheltie's need for protection. Bordetella vaccines are usually given in a nasal spray, although injectable vaccines are also available.

Leptospirosis

Leptospirosis, or "lepto," is caused by bacteria that attack the kidneys. Spread in the urine of infected animals, it causes vomiting, convulsions, vision problems, and eventual kidney failure. Although several different strains of the disease occur, it is rare.

Unfortunately, vaccination is not very effective against the most common strain of the disease. Because serious reactions to the vaccine are not uncommon in dogs, many veterinarians and owners choose not to vaccinate against lepto when risk of exposure is low. If vaccination seems advisable for your Sheltie, consider having the vaccine given separately from any others, and stay at the clinic for half an hour or so after the shot is given in case your dog has a negative reaction to it. If he does, subsequent reactions may be more severe, so do not vaccinate for lepto again, and be sure that this information is included in your dog's veterinary records.

Bacterial diseases are often spread through sneezing or coughing, so vaccination is sometimes advised for dogs who will be regularly exposed to other canines at doggy day care, dog parks, or during shows and other events.

Lyme Disease

Lyme disease is a bacterial disease transmitted by ticks, particularly the tiny deer tick. It causes generalized illness in animals and humans. In the United States, Lyme disease is found primarily in Atlantic and Pacific coast states and in parts of the Midwest. Although both dogs and human beings are susceptible to Lyme disease, you cannot get it directly from your dog. Lyme disease is spread by ticks that ingest the bacteria when they feed on the blood of infected animals and then transmit the bacteria to subsequent hosts through bites.

Lyme disease in dogs is usually diagnosed when the disease causes lameness, pain, and sometimes swelling in one or more joints. Other signs of the disease may include fever, lack of appetite, dehydration, lethargy, and swollen lymph nodes. If caught early, Lyme disease in dogs can usually be cured with antibiotics. Left untreated, Lyme disease becomes chronic, causing crippling arthritis and possible kidney damage.

Most veterinarians do not recommend routine vaccination for Lyme disease when risk of exposure is low, and some believe the vaccine is ineffective in any case. Talk to your vet about current recommendations for your area and your Sheltie's level of risk. If you and your dog spend time where ticks are active, ask about tick preventives, and check both your dog and yourself thoroughly after every outing. (See also "Ticks" and "How to Remove a Tick.")

Parainfluenza

Parainfluenza is a viral infection of the respiratory tract that causes symptoms similar to flu in people. Puppies usually receive a series of three vaccinations, often in combination with other vaccines.

Parvovirus

Parvovirus, commonly known as "parvo," is caused by a highly contagious virus that attacks the intestinal tract, heart muscle, and white blood cells. Signs of parvo include severe and distinctively foul-smelling diarrhea, vomiting, high fever, loss of appetite, and depression. Parvovirus is shed in the feces of infected dogs and is easily transported on shoes, paws, and clothing. Because parvo is impervious to most disinfectants and to extreme temperatures, it is very difficult to eliminate once it enters an area and can remain a threat to unvaccinated dogs for a long time. Even with intensive veterinary care, many dogs die within two or three days of showing initial signs of the disease. Parvo is especially devastating in puppies, and those who survive often suffer lifelong heart problems.

Puppies are usually given a series of three parvo vaccinations, and boosters are recommended on varying schedules for adults, especially seniors.

Rabies

Rabies is a viral disease that can attack the central nervous system of any mammal, including humans. Endemic in populations of wild animals in North America and elsewhere, rabies is spread through the saliva of infected animals, usually by way of a bite. Prevention is critical because once symptoms appear, rabies is always fatal. As a result, pets are required to be vaccinated against rabies in the United States, Canada, and some other countries. Countries that are free of rabies quarantine incoming animals.

Rabies can appear in one of two forms. The form that most of us are familiar with is *furious* rabies, which causes aggression and foaming at the mouth. People usually avoid animals that display these observable behaviors, thus reducing their chances of contracting the disease. However, when affected with the *dumb* form of the disease, animals may not display obvious symptoms right away; they

Drugs and the MDR1 Mutation

Some dogs, particularly many "collie-type" dogs like the Shetland Sheepdog, are sensitive to certain drugs. Researchers have identified a genetic mutation, known as the multi-drug resistance, or MDR1, mutation, as the source of the sensitivity. Adverse reactions can cause seizures, other neurological complications, and death. Dogs with the MDR1 mutation may react to the following drugs:

- **acepromazine:** a tranquilizer and preanesthetic agent, acepromazine causes extreme, prolonged sedation
- **butorphanol:** an analgesic and preanesthetic agent, butorphanol causes extreme, prolonged sedation
- **ivermectin:** used to prevent and treat heartworm and to treat mange and other parasitic infections, ivermectin may cause seizures, drooling, stumbling, other neurological complications, coma, and possibly death in MDR1 dogs
- **loperamide:** an active ingredient in antidiarrheal medication, loperamide causes neurological toxicity and should never be given to MDR1 dogs
- **milbemycin, moxidectin, and selamectin:** these active ingredients in several heartworm medications are said to be safe for MDR1 dogs at normal dosages, but toxic at higher dosages; some owners report toxic effects after prolonged use at normal dosages
- **vincristine, vinblastine, and doxorubicin:** these chemotherapy agents may cause decreased blood cell counts, anorexia, vomiting, and diarrhea

Researchers also recommend caution in giving the following drugs to dogs with the MDR1 mutation, because they may metabolize them differently and have a variety of adverse reactions to them at normal dosages: domperidone, etoposide, mitoxantrone, ondansetron, paclitaxel, and rifampicin.

A simple cheek-swab test is now available to determine whether an individual dog has the MDR1 mutation. To obtain the test kit, contact Washington State University College of Veterinary Medicine, Veterinary Clinical Pharmacology Laboratory, PO Box 609, Pullman, WA 99163-0609, 509-335-3745, website: www.vetmed.wsu.edu, e-mail: VCPL@vetmed.wsu.edu. Be sure to discuss the test results with your vet.

will eventually experience paralysis, usually beginning with the lower jaw and spreading through the limbs and vital organs until the animal dies. Aside from contracting rabies through a bite, the disease can be transmitted through saliva deposited on broken skin (rabies can enter the body from a lick to an open scratch, wound, or mucus membrane). If you think you or your dog have been exposed to rabies, seek medical attention immediately.

Puppies should be vaccinated against rabies at three to four months of age and then given booster shots in subsequent years. As a result of concerns about the negative effects of excessive vaccination, research is under way to determine the long-term efficacy of rabies vaccines. Until the results are in, though, your dog must be revaccinated according to the laws where you live—in the United States, rabies boosters are required annually by some states, while others have moved to a three-year requirement.

CONTROLLING PARASITES

Your Sheltie, like all animals, is a potential host for a variety of parasites, which are organisms that take their nutrition from other living creatures. Fortunately, you can keep your dog and your home free of these creepy critters by utilizing good preventive care and by responding quickly if you see or suspect that your dog has picked up any unwanted passengers.

Heartworm Disease

Heartworms are parasitic worms that infest the heart of their host animal. When a mosquito bites an infected animal, it ingests heartworm microfilaria (microscopic larvae) present in the animal's blood. Upon biting its next victim, the mosquito injects some of the microfilaria, which then travel through the animal's blood vessels to the heart, where they mature and reproduce. The number and size of individual heartworms increase, eventually filling the space available and causing congestive heart failure.

Two types of tests are used to diagnose heartworm infections. A filter test (or Knott's test) involves microscopic examination of blood to see whether microfilaria are present; if they are not, the animal is diagnosed as heartworm negative. A more commonly used test detects adult heartworm antigens, substances that stimulate the creation of antibodies in the blood. Antigen tests are more expensive than filter tests but more accurate in detecting heartworms since sterile adult or one-sex-only infestations produce no microfilaria.

Heartworm larvae take about six months to develop into reproducing adults, so a test done within six months of initial infection will appear negative. Most vets therefore recommend that puppies be tested for heartworm infection at seven months (in case they were infected during their first eight weeks), and that adults be tested every year or two even if they take preventives because, although modern medications are highly effective, none are perfect.

Signs of heartworm disease often don't appear until at least a year after initial infection. The first indication is often a soft, deep cough, especially after exercise. An infected dog may also lose weight and become weak and lethargic, and some may spit up blood.

Heartworm disease is now found in dogs throughout the United States, as well as in other countries. Fortunately, effective preventive medications are available. Be aware that some Shelties are sensitive to ingredients in some heartworm medications and other drugs, and be sure your vet knows about the possibility. Puppies should be started on regular heartworm prevention at eight weeks of age. If you have an adult Sheltie who has not been given heartworm preventive, have him tested before you begin— preventive medications can kill a dog who is already infected with adult heartworms. Many vets now recommend that dogs be given heartworm preventive year round. Several brands are available; most are given once a month, and, as an added plus, most eliminate several types of intestinal worms as well.

Treatment for heartworm disease begins with drug therapy to kill the adult heartworms. The patient must be kept quiet during treatment to prevent complications or potential death as the dead worms are flushed from the heart. Once the adult worms are killed, follow-up treatment is often used to eliminate any microfilaria that remain.

Intestinal Parasites

Many species of parasites occupy the digestive system of dogs and other animals. Although a few parasites live quietly and cause no obvious problems, many cause diarrhea, bloody stools, weight loss, dry coat, and/or vomiting. Some parasites can even lie dormant in your dog's body in egg or larval stages, only to become activated when their host is under stress or, in the case of roundworms, until they can infest soon-to-be-born puppies.

Some intestinal parasites are visible to the naked eye, but many are microscopic. Although some are fairly easy to eliminate with the right medication, others are more tenacious, so you may have to treat your dog more than once to eliminate them. Most pet dogs should be checked annually. If your Sheltie spends a lot of time where other animals travel, wild or domestic, two or three checks a year would be better.

You may occasionally see worms in your dog's stool, especially if you have a young puppy. Don't panic—worms are disturbing but do not constitute a medical emergency. Grab a plastic bag, grit your teeth, collect a specimen, and take it to your vet. She will identify the parasite and prescribe the right product to eradicate it. Don't waste money and time, or risk your dog's health, with over-the-counter dewormers or home remedies—many are ineffective, and some are dangerous, especially when combined with certain other products. Your vet can also advise you on how to prevent the

To prevent the spread of parasites, pick up after your dog in your yard and in public places.

How to Collect a Fecal Sample

Collecting fecal specimens to take to your vet may not be the most pleasant aspect of owning a Sheltie, but it is an essential part of responsible care. And really, it's no harder than cleaning up your backyard or picking up after your dog in public places. Here's how to make the job quick and easy. Insert your hand into a small- to medium-sized plastic bag or glove. (If you use a zip-lock bag, turn it inside out first so the zipper will be usable.) Find a fresh dropping, and pick up a little piece with your gloved hand—your vet doesn't need much. Pull the open edge of the bag or glove off your hand, trapping the sample inside. Zip up the bag, or tie a knot in it, and get it to your vet as soon as possible.

spread of the parasite to other pets, including those of other people.

Be aware that some parasites will happily inhabit humans, so until your dog gets the all-clear from your vet, wash your hands with soap and hot water after handling him and after performing "poop patrol" in your yard. Teach your children to do the same. To prevent the spread of parasites, remove dog feces from your backyard at least once a week (more often if you have more than one dog), pick up after your dog in public places, and avoid walking your Sheltie in places where other dog owners have not practiced fecal responsibility.

Coccidia

Coccidia are protozoa (single-celled organisms) that attack the small intestine. A healthy adult dog may show no signs of infection, but in a young, unhealthy, or stressed animal they can cause coccidiosis, signs of which may include intestinal cramping, bloody diarrhea, dehydration, anemia, and weight loss. Stress may trigger an outbreak of coccidiosis in a dog who has been infected but asymptomatic.

Coccidia infections can be difficult to diagnose. They are usually treated with such drugs as sulfadimethoxine and trimethoprim-sulfadiazine, which prevent the protozoa from reproducing, giving the dog's immune system time to develop a defensive response to eventually eliminate the coccidia. Elimination of coccidia usually takes from one to three weeks.

Giardia

Giardia are single-celled parasites that attach themselves to the lining of the small intestine. They may cause no ill effects and go undetected in a healthy adult Sheltie, but in a puppy or in a dog with an impaired immune system, they can cause problems. Giardia, which can affect people as well as dogs and other animals, are shed in the feces of infected animals. Streams and other water sources are often contaminated with giardia, so try not to let your Sheltie drink unpurified water on walks or hikes.

Signs include soft, mucous-coated, light-colored stools or extremely foul-smelling diarrhea, as well as weight loss and listlessness. Your vet can diagnose giardia through microscopic examination of a fecal specimen and prescribe appropriate medication.

Hookworms

Hookworms are tiny worms that can cause your dog to become very ill. If a bitch has not been kept free of parasites, she may give her puppies hookworms while they are *in utero* or nursing. Chronic hookworm infection scars the lining of the intestine and may cause anemia, diarrhea, weight loss, and weakness. A heavy or long-term infection can be fatal, especially in a puppy who has not had good pre- and post-natal care.

Dogs (and people) can also acquire hookworms by walking on soil contaminated with hookworm larvae, which burrow through the skin and into the bloodstream. Once in the bloodstream, they ride to the small intestine, where they attach themselves with hooks, suck blood from the tissue, and mature.

Hookworm infection is diagnosed by the appearance of microscopic eggs in feces. Your vet can prescribe an effective treatment.

Roundworms

Roundworms are very common in dogs, especially young puppies (including those who have had excellent care). Roundworms look like white strings of spaghetti about 8 inches (20 cm) long. They live in the host animal's intestines and stomach, where they eat food the host has ingested.

Roundworms are often passed with feces, and a dog with a heavy infection may develop diarrhea and may vomit worms as well. If enough worms are present, the puppy may become malnourished as the worms steal his food. An infected pup may become lethargic, and if the infection is allowed to continue, he may stop eating. A puppy with roundworms typically also sports a pot belly.

Roundworms are easy to eliminate, so if you think your Sheltie has them, take a fecal sample to your vet for verification and treatment. Roundworms can be transmitted to people, so wash your hands after handling your pup, and teach your children to do the same.

Tapeworms

Tapeworms are white worms that have easily seen body segments. Although they can grow to more than 2 feet (60 cm) in length and occasionally show up in feces, tapeworms are more often identified by tiny rice-like segments that break off from the worm and stick to fur around the animal's anus.

Tapeworms require an intermediate host, such as a flea, rodent, or rabbit, to reproduce. If your Sheltie eats an infected critter and

Puppies can be severely affected by internal parasites.

ingests tapeworm larvae, they will travel to his intestines and develop into adult tapeworms. A long-term tapeworm infection can cause weight loss and other health problems.

General-purpose dewormers do not eliminate tapeworms, so if you see any suspicious rice-like particles around your dog's anus (or, less commonly, lengths of tapeworm in his feces), talk to your vet for proper diagnosis and treatment.

Whipworms

Whipworms are tiny worms that look like bits of thread with one enlarged end. They live in the large intestine, and they may cause colitis and diarrhea, which can lead to dehydration and other problems if left untreated.

Because they usually occur in small numbers, whipworms can be tricky to diagnose, sometimes requiring examination of several fecal specimens taken over several days. Stools from a dog with whipworms often have a mucous-like coating, which can be helpful in diagnosing this infection. Once diagnosed, your vet can prescribe effective treatment.

External Parasites

External parasites, such as tiny fleas, ticks, and mange mites, live on the surface of their host. They can be big trouble for your Sheltie unless you fight back. Bites they inflict not only make their victims uncomfortable, but also spread a number of diseases. The itching of these bites can also cause dogs to scratch themselves raw, opening the way for infections and leading to chronic skin irritations and hair loss. Fortunately, excellent products are available to enable you to protect your pet from these pests. As in the fight against internal parasites, your veterinarian can recommend specific products that are best for your situation.

If your Sheltie experiences any unexplained hair loss, itching, or skin irritation, take him to your veterinarian for diagnosis and treatment before the problem gets worse. (See also discoid lupus erythematosus in "Autoimmune Diseases.") Some parasites will attack people and other animals, so if any human member of your household experiences similar symptoms, see a doctor and tell them about your dog.

Fleas

Fleas are small insects clad in hard black or reddish-
brown protective shells. They eat blood, and because
they move quickly and can jump, they're hard to catch.
They can carry diseases and tapeworm larvae, and in a
puppy or small Sheltie, a large infestation of fleas can
cause anemia. Fleas can drive your dog crazy with
itching, and if your Sheltie is allergic to flea saliva,
even a single bite can cause a scratching frenzy that
can lead to skin irritation and open sores. All in all,
fleas are bad news.

To control and prevent fleas, it's important to
understand their life cycle. Fleas deposit their eggs onto
the skin or hair of the host pet. The eggs then drop off
during normal activities in places the host animal frequents. The
greatest concentration of eggs is usually where the pet spends the
most time or where he is very active: near beds, furniture, stairs,
doors and windows, and the like. Under favorable conditions,
eggs hatch into larvae within two weeks. Pupal stages may last as
long as 140 days. Flea larvae, which look like teensy maggots, eat
the blood-rich feces of adult fleas. They molt twice as they grow,
then form a hard little cocoon (pupa) from which they eventually
emerge as adult fleas.

In some environments, the war against fleas (and ticks) is
perpetual due to a favorable climate and other factors. However,
if you only see parasites on your Sheltie or in his environment
occasionally, flea preventives are not necessary. Constant exposure
to toxic chemicals may have negative long-term side effects, so
avoid using them when possible. Talk to your vet and assess your
individual situation to make an informed decision.

If you do find fleas on your dog, or in your home, yard, or
vehicle, act quickly to prevent a population explosion. Beware
of over-the-counter products—some are not very effective, and
some are dangerous, especially when combined with one another.
Don't bother with flea and tick collars; they are not very effective
and can cause respiratory distress in some dogs. Your veterinarian
can recommend relatively safe products to eliminate fleas, eggs,
and larvae in your home, yard, and vehicle. As with all drugs and
chemicals, follow directions, observe warnings, and avoid products
that may adversely affect your dog.

Mites

Mites are microscopic parasitic arthropods, relatives of spiders and ticks. Several species of mites can live on the skin of dogs, eating skin debris, hair follicles, and tissue, causing various types of mange. Dogs with mange typically develop itchy, flaky, crusty, bald spots, and often scratch themselves raw, opening the way for bacteria, viruses, fungi, and other parasites.

Three types of mange mites attack dogs:

- **Demodex Mites:** Demodex mites live on many healthy puppies and dogs without causing problems. Some puppies, though, are less resistant and, as a result, the mites they carry reproduce more rapidly than normal, causing a condition called demodectic mange, or demodex. Seen most often in puppies from three months to a year old, demodex characteristically causes thinning of the hair around the eyes, mouth, and front legs. Demodex usually resolves (cures itself) within two or three months without causing major problems, but some puppies develop oozing sores and crusty skin, which eventually causes hair loss over large areas of the body. So, it's important to seek veterinary diagnosis and treatment at the first signs of a problem. Demodex occasionally develops in adult dogs whose immune systems are unable to control the normally benign mites due to such factors as cancer, hypothyroidism, adrenal gland diseases, or certain medications. Poor nutrition or other elements of poor care can also cause stress that leads to adult-onset demodex, so this type of mange is not uncommon in dogs abandoned to shelters or rescue programs. To control demodectic mange in adults, the underlying cause must be resolved so that the immune system can recover.

- **Sarcoptic Mites:** The mites that cause sarcoptic mange (scabies) burrow under their victim's skin to lay eggs, from which larvae quickly emerge, develop into adult mites, and lay more eggs. As you might imagine, scabies causes intense itching, oozing sores, crusty ear tips, secondary infections, and hair loss that begins on the ears, elbows, legs, and face, and eventually covers the dog's body. Quick veterinary response is critical not only for the dog's sake, but to prevent the mites from spreading to the human family. Unfortunately, sarcoptic mange is often misdiagnosed as allergic dermatitis because the burrowing mites often don't show up in skin

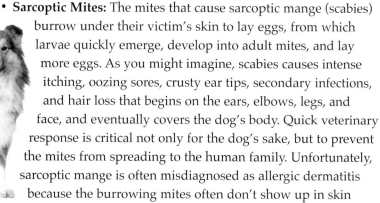

scrapings. Because it's so hard to find the mites themselves, some veterinarians prefer to treat for scabies before considering allergic dermatitis. For Shelties, that can be a problem because the drug of choice for treating scabies is ivermectin, which can cause potentially lethal reactions in some dogs. (See "Drugs and the MDR1 Mutation," and either have your dog tested for sensitivity before using ivermectin, or insist on a different drug. Also read about food allergies in Chapter 4.)

- **Cheyletiella:** Cheyletiella are tiny white mites that look like dandruff moving around on the dog's head, neck, and back—hence the common name "walking dandruff" for this type of mange. Although they cause mild itching in puppies, and they are easily passed from one dog to another, and even to people, cheyletiellosis is easily cured with proper diagnosis and treatment.

Ringworm

Despite its name, ringworm is a highly contagious fungal infection, not a worm. It does, however, typically begin by causing a small round hairless area with scaly skin in the center, and it spreads quickly and easily from one pet to another and to people.

Always check your dog for fleas, mites, and ticks after he's been playing outdoors.

Like all fungal infections, ringworm is very difficult to treat. Don't waste time or money on over-the-counter or home remedies that will most likely be ineffective and just give the infection time to become better established. Your veterinarian can prescribe more effective drugs and tell you how to prevent the infection from spreading to other members of your household and neighborhood.

Ticks

Ticks are small arthropods (relatives of spiders and mites) that eat blood. Like fleas, ticks carry a number of diseases, including babesiosis, anaplasmosis, ehrlichia, East Coast fever, relapsing fever, Rocky Mountain spotted fever, and Lyme disease. They are frequently found in fields and woods, but have no qualms about hitching rides on animals and people, so you may also find them in your yard and even your home.

Unfed ticks are round and flat, with eight tiny legs and a teensy little head sticking out from their bodies. After they eat, though,

How to Remove a Tick

Your Sheltie's lush coat can make ticks hard to find, but if he spends time in the woods or other places populated by the little bloodsuckers, it's important to try.

Systematically part sections of your dog's coat to the skin, working from front to back, and paying special attention to hiding places like ears, armpits, and the groin area. If you find a tick that has not yet bitten into the flesh, pick it up with a tissue and either flush it down the toilet or seal it into a plastic bag and put it in the garbage. If the tick has already attached itself to the flesh, perform the following steps for proper removal:

- Dab the tick with a cotton ball soaked in alcohol, iodine, or a strong saline solution to loosen its grip.
- Grasp the tick's body firmly (as close to the head as possible) with a tick remover or tweezers and pull it straight out. Don't twist or squeeze—you may leave the head behind or force disease-filled fluid into the victim.
- If you remove a very small tick, show it to your veterinarian for identification. Tiny deer ticks carry Lyme disease, which affects people as well as dogs.
- Unless you pulled its head off, the tick is still alive, so handle it carefully. Drop it into alcohol, flush it down the toilet, or seal it into a plastic bag for disposal.
- You should see a small hole in the skin after you remove the tick. If you see a black spot, you've left the head. Either way, keep an eye on the area for a few days, and call your vet if the area becomes inflamed or a rash develops.
- Clean the area with alcohol or antibacterial cleanser, dry, and apply antibacterial ointment.
- Wash your hands and tools with antibacterial soap.

Note the date of the bite. Tick-borne illnesses take time to incubate and can be hard to diagnose, so a record of the date of any bite may be useful if your dog becomes ill.

they swell up and look like beans with legs. Deer ticks are tiny and very hard to spot until after they've eaten.

If you live or travel where there are ticks, check your dog frequently for these unwanted passengers, and remove any you find. (See also "How to Remove a Tick.") If you find a lot of ticks, or find them frequently, ask your vet about safe products to repel and kill ticks during warm weather.

HORMONES, HEALTH, AND BEHAVIOR

The American Shetland Sheepdog Association (ASSA) encourages owners to spay or neuter all but the very best Shelties in terms of breed type, temperament, and individual and genetic health. Responsible breeders, rescue organizations, and shelters require all pets to be altered (spayed or neutered). The American Kennel Club (AKC), various local and national humane groups, and informed dog trainers, rescuers, veterinarians, and owners also strongly encourage altering.

Why the big fuss? Visit your local animal shelter, or call a Sheltie rescue organization, and you'll soon realize that numerous Shelties and other wonderful dogs lose their homes each year. Many of them are eventually euthanized for lack of homes. Responsible dog ownership includes a commitment to the welfare of any puppies your pet produces. That means that your Sheltie shouldn't give birth to or sire a single puppy unless you are willing to care for that puppy throughout his life if necessary.

Spaying and Neutering

Pet overpopulation isn't the only reason to spay or neuter your Sheltie though. Spaying (removal of the ovaries and uterus) eliminates the risks of pregnancy and whelping, prevents life-threatening cancers or infections of the uterus and ovaries, and, if done before a bitch has her first heat or at least before she's two years old, greatly reduces her risk of developing mammary tumors later in life. Spaying also makes a bitch easier to live with because she doesn't experience the hormonal swings of an intact female, nor will she attract canine Casanovas to your door.

Some people have the mistaken idea that having a litter will calm a bitch down and make her sweeter and more loving. But the truth is that training, exercise, and maturity lead to calmer behavior, not motherhood. Having puppies will focus your pet's attention away from her human family, and she may become very protective of the puppies. Even when she doesn't have puppies, fluctuating hormone levels can make an unspayed female moody and sometimes aggressive. Spaying makes for a more emotionally stable pet.

Neutering (castration) will not only keep your dog from siring puppies, with or without your permission, but will also minimize some of the behaviors that people find annoying in male dogs, including territorial urine marking and roaming in search of females. An unneutered male dog is a mess when he detects a bitch in heat—which he can do from miles away. He will refuse to eat, whine, pace the floor, howl, and slobber. He'll be distracted and may become aggressive with other males. Neutering won't make your dog wimpy, but will probably make him more tolerant of other male dogs. Neutering also offers health benefits, preventing testicular cancer and greatly reducing the risk of prostate problems.

Spaying or neutering won't change your Sheltie's basic personality. On the contrary, it will eliminate the urges brought on by hormones and let positive traits dominate your pet's personality. Altering won't make your dog fat, either. Too much food and too little exercise are the main causes of obesity.

All in all, there are far more reasons to have your Sheltie spayed or neutered than there are to keep her or his breeding potential intact.

HEALTH ISSUES IN SHETLAND SHEEPDOGS

Don't let this section of the book scare you—most Shetland Sheepdogs are healthy. On the other hand, all living beings have certain vulnerabilities based on ancestry (including humans). Knowing about health problems to which your Sheltie may be susceptible will improve your ability to safeguard his health and help you know what to look for if your dog becomes ill.

Allergies

Allergies occur when an animal's immune system releases histamines to defend the body against an allergen, a substance it perceives as a threat. Although

Just as in humans, allergies are relatively common in pets. Pesticides or lawn chemicals are potential allergens that can cause itchy, irritated skin at the site of contact.

many Shelties have no allergies, allergies are quite common in dogs. Dogs with inhalant allergies itch and also often have oily, raw, and infected skin. Food allergies typically cause a range of allergic reactions, including itching, inflamed ears, head shaking, excessive licking (obvious when lovely white toes and feet turn rusty pink from proteins in the saliva), face and head rubbing, flatulence, diarrhea, vomiting, sneezing, breathing difficulty, behavioral changes, and seizures.

Tracking down the source of an allergy can be quite a challenge. Allergies can develop over time, and your Sheltie may develop an allergic reaction to something that didn't bother him before. Although allergies cannot be "cured," their effects can often be controlled. Here are some things to try if your Sheltie develops an allergy:

- **Control your dog's diet and environment.** Once identified, remove or avoid the offending source if possible. For example, if your dog is allergic to something in his food (corn, wheat, and soy are common canine allergens), try a new food. If he goes into a scratching frenzy whenever you use carpet deodorizer, stop using the product. If he's allergic to grass, keep him off the lawn as much as possible. HEPA air filters are highly effective for

reducing airborne allergens in your home.

- **Treat the symptoms.** Antihistamines can help, although they make some dogs sleepy. Corticosteroids such as cortisone, dexamethasone, or prednisone may reduce itching, but long-term use can suppress the immune system or cause diabetes or seizures. Even short-term use can stimulate hunger and thirst, causing your dog to gain weight and urinate more often. As always, consult your vet before giving your dog any medication, including over-the-counter medicines, herbal remedies, or other "natural" healing products.
- **Supplement your dog's diet**. Make sure that your dog's diet includes essential fatty acids, which are natural anti-inflammatories.

If you can't identify the source of your dog's discomfort within a reasonable amount of time, have him tested by a veterinary dermatologist. If the allergen can be identified but cannot be removed from your dog's environment, immunotherapy (which consists of a series of allergy shots) may help, although it can take months to show positive results, and some dogs do not respond to it at all.

Autoimmune Diseases

A properly working immune system is an animal's first defense against invasion from outside organisms that cause illness. When bacteria or viruses enter the body, this defensive response is necessary and appropriate. Unfortunately, like any complex system, the immune system can malfunction, mistaking the body's own tissue for a threat. If that happens, the body has an autoimmune response, attacking and rejecting the body's own tissue. In some cases, the target is a specific type of tissue; in others, the immune system attacks multiple tissue targets. When the immune system attacks the body in which it lives, the animal is said to have autoimmune disease. A few types of autoimmune disease occur with some regularity in Shelties.

Discoid lupus erythematosus (DLE) is an autoimmune dermatitis that causes lesions and hair loss on the face in a characteristic "butterfly pattern" over the nose. DLE appears to be inherited, and although it cannot be cured, it can usually be controlled with drugs that suppress the body's immune response.

Autoimmune lymphocytic thyroiditis, the inherited form of

thyroid disease, also occurs in some Shelties, but thyroid disease is not always genetic. (For more on the signs and treatment of canine thyroid disease, see "Thyroid Disease.")

Canine Cancers

Cancers, which are characterized by uncontrolled reproduction of cells and their invasion of nearby body structures, affect dogs as frequently as they affect people. Metastatic cancers spread to distant parts of the animal and are particularly deadly. Although young dogs can get cancer, it's more common in dogs older than seven years.

It may be possible through surgery to remove a tumor or reduce its size. Chemotherapy drugs may be used to inhibit or kill cancer cells, and in some cases radiation therapy is used. Nutritional and alternative therapies (see "Alternative Therapies") can promote overall physical and emotional health, enhancing the dog's ability to fight cancer. Some canine cancers have a fairly high cure rate; others do not. If your Sheltie is diagnosed with cancer, his prognosis will depend on the type of cancer and how early it was diagnosed, as well as on your dog's age, general health, and other factors.

Be proactive on your Sheltie's behalf. Some canine cancers can be prevented. Spayed females have no risk of ovarian or uterine cancer because they no longer have those organs, and if they are spayed before their first heat, their risk of mammary (breast) cancer is much lower than otherwise. Neutered males cannot develop testicular cancer. Your lifestyle also affects your dog's health. Long-term exposure to chemicals inside and outside your home can increase his cancer risk, and there is evidence that dogs who live with smokers are at risk for lung cancer. If you won't quit for yourself, do it for your dog.

If you find any unusual lump, growth, or swelling on your dog, or if you notice unexplained limping, coughing, or other abnormal behaviors, have your vet take a look as soon as possible. Noncancerous fatty tumors are common in older dogs and usually pose no health threat, but if there is a problem, your dog's chances are better with early diagnosis.

Speaking of Cancer

Terminology used to describe and discuss cancers can be confusing. Here are some of the most commonly used terms and what they mean:

- cancer: a malignant, cellular tumor
- neoplasm: an abnormal growth of tissue in animals or plants; a tumor
- tumor: a growth of tissue due to uncontrolled cell multiplication
- benign tumor: a tumor that does not metastasize, or invade other tissue
- malignant tumor: a tumor that contains abnormal cells and invades other tissue (metastasizes)
- carcinoma: a malignant growth of epithelial cells (cells that line the surface of our skin and organs) that often invades surrounding tissue
- sarcoma: a malignant tumor that originates in blood or in connective or lymphatic tissue
- abnormal growth: an abnormal increase in the size of the tissue
- lump: a structure extending beyond the normal surface of the tissue
- metastasize: spread throughout the body

Ear Problems

Compared to some breeds, Shelties suffer relatively few ear problems. Still, those sharp little ears are fairly delicate and susceptible to infection and injury. Knowing the signs of ear and hearing problems will help you catch potential problems early.

Ear Infections

The warm, moist environment of the ear canal is a perfect breeding ground for the bacteria and yeast that cause ear infections. Although Shelties are not as prone to ear infections as are some breeds, you should check your dog's ears once a week for excessive discharge or foul odor. If your Sheltie suffers from allergies, be especially vigilant.

If you think your dog has an ear infection, don't waste time and money on home remedies or over-the-counter cures. Effective treatment requires accurate diagnosis, and the wrong medication can make an infection worse, causing your dog more pain and possibly resulting in permanent hearing loss. Through microscopic examination of ear swabs, your vet can identify the organism causing the infection and prescribe effective treatment.

Ear Injuries

Ear injuries are not uncommon in dogs, especially dogs like

Shelties who enjoy outdoor activities. That soft fur behind your Sheltie's ears is a lovely hiding place for biting insects and ticks, and a trap for burrs, seeds, and other debris that not only tangle the hair but can poke and irritate the skin or even fall into the ear canal. If you can see the object and remove it easily, that's great. (See also "Ear Care," in Chapter 5). However, if a foreign object is trapped deep in your dog's ear canal or embedded in the skin, have your veterinarian remove it to minimize the risk of further injury or infection. If there is no injury yet, but something is caught tight in the hair around the ear, go to a professional groomer, who can remove it properly.

Occasionally, a hematoma, which is a blood-filled swelling, can occur when an injury breaks a blood vessel in the ear flap, causing it to bleed into surrounding tissue. Although probably uncomfortable for the dog, and definitely not pretty, hematomas of the ear flap don't usually pose any serious health threats. In fact, small hematomas often heal without intervention. Large hematomas, however, require veterinary attention. Typically, minor surgery is performed to reduce swelling, and a small drain may be left in the ear for several days so that the area doesn't refill with fluid.

Knowing how to recognize potential health problems and how to handle them is important to your dog's overall well-being.

179

Animals, especially dogs, also sometimes injure one another's ears. In the case of a serious dog fight or attack, injuries can be severe, but most bite injuries occur by accident during rough play. All bites, to the ears or other areas, pose a high risk of infection because they introduce bacteria from the mouth, so veterinary attention is essential. (See also "First Aid.")

Deafness

Just like people, some dogs born with normal hearing eventually become partially or completely deaf due to old age, or as a result of outside causes such as infection, injury, or exposure to loud noises or to certain chemicals or drugs.

Congenital deafness also occurs in dogs, especially those who lack pigment in some or all of their fur and skin. In other words, congenital deafness is most common in dogs who are white over some or all of their bodies and heads. Being white is not a perfect indicator however—not all white dogs are deaf, and not all deaf dogs have white ears—but it is a clue to possible hearing problems. What does hair color have to do with deafness, you ask? Pigment cells in nonwhite dogs not only color their fur and skin, but also convert sound waves into electrical impulses that are carried to the brain by nerves. When pigment cells are missing from the ear, the nerve endings atrophy and die, and sounds waves that enter the ear go no farther—the dog can't hear. Therefore, Shelties with white heads and, especially, white ears—which is common in homozygous or "double" merle dogs—are often deaf, although white dogs with pigmented skin usually are not. Occasionally, dogs with colored ears lack pigment deep inside the ear and are deaf, but that is less common.

Finding out that your dog is partially or completely deaf can be a shock, but if you're willing to make a few adjustments, the two of you can still live a long, happy life together. Deaf dogs can learn to respond to visual signals in place of verbal commands, and information and resources are readily available to help you as the owner of a deaf dog. (See also "Resources for Owners of Deaf and Blind Dogs.") Just remember that congenitally deaf dogs don't seem to know that they are different from other dogs, and dogs who lose some or all of their hearing later in life don't seem to mind. Best of all, your Sheltie doesn't need to hear you in order to love you.

Hearing Tests: A dog with bilateral deafness is deaf in both

ears, while a dog with unilateral deafness is deaf in only one ear. If you suspect that your dog cannot hear, do some simple tests, with some caveats. If he is unilaterally deaf, you may not learn much because he will use his other ear. In any case, your dog may react to cues other than the sounds themselves, and you won't know the difference. You can make the test a little more accurate by making sounds when your dog is not looking at you or the source of the sound, and by testing him when other pets or small children are elsewhere so he can't cue off their responses. With those cautions in place, you can get some idea about your dog's hearing ability by trying the following:

- jingle keys or coins in your pocket
- squeak a toy in your pocket or behind your back
- call your dog in a normal voice when he is in another room or is not looking at you
- clap your hands or snap your fingers when your dog is not looking at you
- whistle or hum, and watch for a reaction
- ring a bell

If you are really concerned about your Sheltie's hearing, find a vet who is qualified to perform the Brainstem Auditory Evoked Response (BAER) test, which measures electrical activity in the brain in response to clicking sounds in each ear. There are some limitations to the BAER test because it is designed to test hearing in human infants, and it is limited to the frequency range that people normally hear. Because normal dogs can hear higher frequencies than we do, it's possible for a dog who hears very high-pitched sounds to test deaf. Still, the BAER test will indicate whether your dog can hear most of the sounds of daily life, including your voice. The test takes about fifteen minutes, and it is painless and noninvasive.

Eye Disorders

Your Sheltie's sharp little eyes are marvelous, delicate structures, and they are potentially at risk of injury or disease. Most dogs live their whole lives with no eye problems, so don't be unduly alarmed by the information in this section. On the other hand, information is your best tool for safeguarding your dog's vision and eye health.

Your Sheltie's eyes should be bright, and the area around them should be clean and healthy looking. Redness, swelling, cloudiness in the eye, excessive tearing, squinting, face rubbing, or pawing at the face are not normal. If your dog shows any of these signs of trouble, take him to the vet. Don't wait to see if the problem gets better—rapid diagnosis and treatment can prevent a lot of discomfort and may save your dog's vision.

Now let's look at some specific eye problems that occur in Shetland Sheepdogs.

Cataracts

Normally, the eye's lens is transparent. Aging, injury, and disease can cause canine lenses to form opaque spots called cataracts, which may be visible as white or bluish spots on the surface of the eye. Cataracts don't hurt, but they often cover the pupil and impair vision. In time, a cataract can cause total blindness. Most develop slowly, giving the dog (and his owner) time to adapt, and many can be removed, enabling the dog to see again. If corrective surgery is an option for your Sheltie, the sooner it is performed, the better the results are likely to be. If you opt not to have your dog's cataracts removed, your vet will probably prescribe anti-inflammatory eye drops and recommend annual

Resources for Owners of Deaf and Blind Dogs

If your dog is blind or deaf, you may find the following resources helpful:

- The Canine Eye Registry Foundation (CERF) website at http://www.vmdb.org/cerf.html provides information on conditions that affect the eye, and you can search the site for specific information on Shelties.
- The Blind Dogs website at www.blinddogs.com offers information and links related to partial or complete loss of vision in dogs.
- Owners of partially or completely blind dogs discuss issues related to owning and training on the Blinddogs e-mail list at groups.yahoo.com/group/blinddogs.
- For information on the BAER Test for hearing loss, and to locate a BAER test, visit www.lsu.edu/deafness/baersite.htm
- Owners of partially or completely deaf dogs discuss issues related to owning and training dogs with hearing loss on the Deafdogs e-mail at groups.yahoo.com/group/deafdogs.
- The Deaf Dog Education Action Fund (DDEAF) at www. deafdogs.org offers information and links for owners of dogs with partial or complete hearing loss.

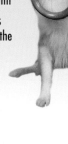

eye exams because many cataracts eventually cause an inner-eye inflammation called lens-induced uveitis (LIU), which can lead to glaucoma, retinal detachment, and other complications.

Cataracts can be caused by injury, disease, old age, or heredity. Some breeds have a high incidence of inherited cataracts, often referred to as juvenile cataracts because they develop long before the dog can be considered old. Inherited cataracts typically are bilateral, meaning that they affect both eyes, although they may not make their initial appearance simultaneously. In addition, inherited cataracts usually progress, or grow, over time.

As your Sheltie ages, he may develop old-age (senile) cataracts. Many geriatric dogs also develop nuclear sclerosis, a hardening of the lens that causes the eye to look cloudy but does not usually affect vision.

Younger dogs, too, can develop cataracts as a result of injury or exposure to airborne dust, excessive heat, chemicals, or radiation, and some dogs develop cataracts because of nutritional deficiencies and exposure to certain drugs or toxins they experienced *in utero* or as very young puppies. Cataracts can also occur as by-products of other types of eye disease, or other diseases, such as diabetes.

Collie Eye Anomaly (CEA)

Despite its name, collie eye anomaly (CEA) is an inherited condition that affects a number of breeds, including the Shetland Sheepdog. In fact, it is sometimes called Sheltie eye syndrome. CEA is actually a complex of defects that includes choroidal hypoplasia, optic disc coloboma/staphyloma, and retinal detachment. These defects may occur alone or in any combination, and although CEA affects both eyes, each eye may show different defects.

CEA is inherited and is present at birth. It can be detected only by a veterinary ophthalmologist using special instruments, which is why responsible Sheltie breeders have their puppies' eyes examined at six to eight weeks of age. After eight weeks, CEA often "goes normal" for a few years, meaning that the dog's eyes appear normal until vision problems show up later.

There is no treatment for CEA. Fortunately, the condition causes no pain or discomfort, and although some dogs with CEA are blind in one or both eyes, most have only minor vision problems that do not limit their ability to live happy, relatively normal lives. Dogs with CEA should not, however, be used for breeding because a parent with mild CEA may have puppies with severe problems.

Merle Ocular Dysgenesis

Homozygous ("double") merles are subject to merle ocular dysgenesis, which involves vision problems due to improper development of the embryonic puppy. (See also "Do Merle Shelties Have Special Problems?" in Chapter 2.)

Heterozygous merles who have inherited only one merle gene have no eye problems directly related to their color. They are, of course, susceptible to all the other eye problems that can affect Shelties of any color.

Eye Infections

Injury or disease can cause your Sheltie's eyes and surrounding tissues to become infected, often indicated by redness, tearing, and itching. If you suspect that an eye infection is developing, take your dog to the vet as soon as possible. Eye infections can be very painful and can quickly cause irreparable, potentially blinding damage. Left untreated, an infection can become an ulcer and, in severe cases, lead to release of fluid of the eye and collapse of the eyeball. If your dog's eye is injured by another animal's claws or

Canine eye problems can escalate quickly, so if you see any signs of trouble, take your dog to a veterinarian right away to prevent further injury and possible loss of vision.

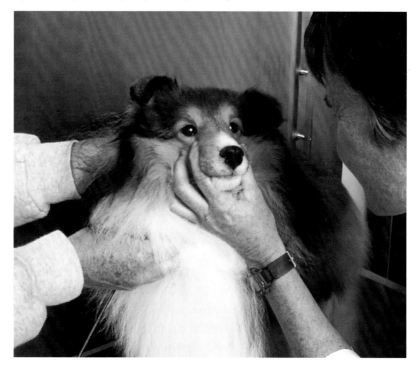

teeth, don't wait for infection to set in before seeing your vet—the massive dose of bacteria introduced by such injuries pretty much guarantees infection if not treated. If the injury to your dog's eye is not obvious, your vet will introduce a sterile staining solution into it. Any break in the corneal surface will take up stain, making the injury visible.

Eye infections are usually treated with antibiotics given in eye drops or ointment. Your vet may also prescribe oral antibiotics and may recommend that your dog wear a restraint collar to keep him from pawing at the eye. If a deep or large ulcer has formed, or if healing takes longer than normal, your vet may draw your dog's nictitating membrane (the white membrane in the inner corner of the eye) across the cornea and temporarily suture it into place to protect the cornea and let it heal.

Conjunctivitis is an infection characterized by congestion and redness of the conjunctiva, which is the pink tissue that lines the inside of the eyelids, covers and protects the front of the eyeball surrounding the cornea, and produces secretions that lubricate the eyes and keep them healthy. Conjunctivitis can be caused by bacteria, viruses, smoke, dirty water, chemicals, foreign matter, allergies, internal disease, or even birth defects. If your Sheltie develops conjunctivitis and you think you know why, remove the cause if possible. Sometimes laboratory tests are necessary to identify the cause. Either way, your veterinarian can prescribe effective treatment.

Eye Injuries

Canine eyes are quite susceptible to destructive inflammations resulting from injury, so any injury to your Sheltie's eyes should be considered serious. Some of the most common eye injuries seen in dogs include the following:

- lacerations of the eyelid or the cornea
- blunt injury to the eyelids or the eye itself from a direct blow
- punctures from thorns, tree branches, or other foreign bodies
- cat claw injuries—these are very common and should *always* receive veterinary attention because claws harbor vast populations of bacteria that can cause devastating infections
- dog bite injuries, especially common in puppies who violate an older dog's space—the extent of the damage may not be obvious even when internal injuries are severe, so any bite to the eye area

should receive veterinary attention as soon as possible

- trauma to the head or eye socket
- chemical injuries from shampoo, cleaners, solvents, paint, mace, and so on
- proptosis, or the popping of the eyeball out of the socket due to trauma, bites, or even massive sinus infections [An eye that has been forced from the socket must be treated by a veterinarian immediately. If possible, have someone drive you to the clinic while you keep your dog quiet and keep the eye and surrounding tissues moist with, in order of preference, sterile saline solution, eye irrigating solution, artificial tears, or water. Do *not* use contact lens solution.]

If you think your dog's eye has been injured, take him to a veterinarian as quickly as you can to prevent further injury and possible loss of vision or loss of the eye itself. Don't let your dog rub at his eye. Put a restraint (Elizabethan) collar on him if you have one, or wrap a towel or blanket snugly around his feet to keep them away from his face. Don't give him any medication, including pain killers, and don't feed him or let him drink in case he has to be anesthetized for treatment. Your vet may refer you to a veterinary ophthalmologist for specialized care once the situation is stabilized.

Some accidents cause such severe damage that the eye must be enucleated (removed). Fortunately, dogs don't worry about how they look, and they adjust well to being blind.

Hot Spots

A hot spot is an area of inflamed skin that may become an open sore as the dog licks and chews to relieve the itching. If you don't groom him regularly, your Sheltie's heavy coat can hold moisture and debris that can irritate his skin and contribute to the formation of hot spots. Other factors that are known to be associated with hot spots include ear infections, irritated anal sacs, lawn and garden products, flea or tick products, harsh or human shampoos (especially if not rinsed thoroughly) and other coat products, cleaning products, fleas, allergies, and neurotic licking and chewing of the skin.

Hot spots usually begin with the loss of some or all of the hair on a patch of skin, which may be swollen, raw, and moist. They can form in a matter of hours and are most common on the legs, paws, flanks, and rump.

To treat a hot spot effectively, you have to treat the sore itself and eliminate or minimize the cause. Your vet will probably clip the hair around the affected area to keep it cleaner and help the sore dry. She also may wrap the injury and/or recommend that your dog wear a restraint ("Elizabethan") collar to prevent further licking and chewing. Don't apply any product to a hot spot without consulting your vet—you may trap infection-causing bacteria in the sore, and your dog may cause more injury licking himself to remove the substance.

Regular grooming can prevent hot spots caused by matted fur. Allergies can often be controlled (see also "Allergies"), and exposure to chemicals can be eliminated or reduced. Shelties tend to be emotionally sensitive dogs, and some develop hot spots in response to factors in their environment (loss of a beloved person or animal, moving to a new home, harsh treatment by a person or animal, and so on). Increased exercise and play times, and lots of supportive attention, often helps reduce stress; if not,

If you don't groom your Sheltie regularly, his heavy coat can hold moisture and debris that can irritate his skin and contribute to the formation of painful hot spots.

your veterinarian should be able to suggest additional therapies to solve the problem.

Thyroid Disease

The thyroid gland lies just below the larynx in your dog's throat. A healthy thyroid gland produces hormones that control growth, development, and the metabolism of proteins, carbohydrates, and lipids (fats). If insufficient thyroid hormone is produced, the dog suffers from hypothyroidism, or "low thyroid," which can have negative effects on the body and emotions.

Hyperthyroidism (the production of too much thyroid hormone) is rare in dogs and is usually associated with cancer when it does occur. Autoimmune lymphocytic thyroiditis, the inherited form of thyroid disease, affects some families of Shelties.

The effects of hypothyroidism can be subtle and hard to detect, but may include some or all of the following signs: hair loss, lethargy, weight gain or obesity, inflamed ears, abnormally cool skin, itching, or inflamed, crusty, or scaly skin. It has also been linked to the development of corneal dystrophy, which can cause partial or complete blindness, and to behavioral problems, including aggression. Hypothyroidism can be difficult to diagnose because hormone levels can be affected by other diseases, and because the signs of thyroid disease may also indicate other problems. Thyroid disease often develops slowly, and early changes in thyroid levels may be too small to detect, so it may be necessary to test more than once at intervals. If your dog has persistent signs of thyroid disease and other conditions have been ruled out, have him retested in six to twelve months.

Laboratory analysis of blood samples is used to detect thyroid disease. Blood should be drawn when your dog is otherwise healthy, and he should not take steroids, nonsteroidal anti-inflammatories, or anti-seizure drugs prior to the test (check with your veterinarian to determine how long he should be drug-free before the blood draw). Many vets and owners opt for the less expensive, less complicated T4 test, but unfortunately it's not very reliable. For more accurate results, ask your vet to do a complete blood panel that measures total T4, free T4 (the usable T4 in the blood), TGAA (thyroglobulin autoantibodies), cTSH (canine thyroid stimulating hormone), and sometimes T3 and free T3. You will have to pay a little more and wait a little longer for results, but diagnosis will be more accurate, enabling you to begin any necessary treatment that much sooner.

Happily, treatment for hypothyroidism is relatively inexpensive and usually controls hormone levels effectively. Your vet will probably want to retest your dog after a month or two of treatment to be sure the dosage is correct. Once the proper dosage is determined, your dog should be retested once or twice a year.

ALTERNATIVE THERAPIES

Many veterinarians and pet owners have become concerned in recent years about the possible negative effects of excessive use of vaccinations and other drugs. As a result, there has been increased interest in alternative, complementary, or holistic approaches to canine health care, used alone or often in conjunction with more traditional medicine. Alternative approaches vary in philosophy and method, but they are all based on the idea that bodily systems work together to affect physical and emotional health.

Alternative approaches to canine health care include the following modalities.

Acupuncture

Acupuncture involves the use of needles, massage, heat, and lasers to stimulate the release of hormones, endorphins, and other chemical substances to help the body fight off pain and disease.

Chiropractic

Chiropractic is based on the belief that proper alignment of the skeletal system, particularly the spine, is critical to the functioning of the nervous system and overall good health. Chiropractic care can be very beneficial, especially if your Sheltie is very active, but a practitioner who lacks proper training in canine anatomy and

Chiropractic care can benefit dogs who suffer from musculoskeletal problems related to disease or injury, especially if they are very active.

physiology can cause serious injury. If you want to try chiropractic treatment for your Sheltie, find a licensed veterinarian who is also trained in chiropractic.

Herbal Therapy

Herbal therapy involves the use of herbs to promote good health and treat disease. Herbal therapy can be highly effective, but the use of herbs also requires caution. Don't confuse "natural" with "safe"—some herbs are extremely toxic, and some that are safe to use in small doses can be fatal in larger amounts. Herbs should be used only under the supervision of someone who is very knowledgeable about their properties.

Homeopathy

Homeopathy is based on the idea that "like treats like," and homeopathic remedies are generally minute doses of substances that, in larger doses, would cause symptoms like those of the disease. As with other nontraditional forms of treatment, if you are interested in trying homeopathic remedies for your Sheltie, be sure that the practitioner is qualified to work with dogs, preferably with a degree in veterinary science. The Academy of Veterinary

Homeopathy certifies and monitors veterinarians who are trained in classical homeopathic medicine. See www.theAVH.org for more information.

Nutritional Therapy

Nutritional therapy uses the addition and omission of specific foods and supplements to promote better health and to treat certain conditions. Grain-free diets, alternate protein sources such as venison or bison, or supplements believed to support the proper functioning of specific bodily systems may replace more conventional foods, fillers, and chemical preservatives. Other common dog-food ingredients may also be removed from the dog's diet.

Finding Alternative Practitioners

Although many alternative practitioners are highly qualified, there are some quacks out there, so be cautious about who you allow to treat your dog. A licensed veterinarian trained in holistic or alternative techniques combines the best of both worlds, and some well-qualified lay practitioners also do a lot of good. But inappropriate treatment can delay accurate diagnosis and effective therapies, sometimes with disastrous effects.

To find a good alternative practitioner, contact your vet, local shelters, rescue programs, dog breeders, and dog clubs, as well as your own relatives, friends, and neighbors. Ask why people like their practitioner, and find out if there's anyone they would avoid and why. The yellow pages or Internet may be helpful, but try to visit the practice and meet the staff before you hand your dog over for treatment. You can also get information from the American Holistic Veterinary Medical Association (AHVMA) website at www.ahvma.com.

EMERGENCY CARE AND FIRST AID

No matter how carefully you protect your Sheltie, an emergency can occur in a heartbeat. If you know what to do and where to put your hands on equipment and supplies, you and your dog will fare much better in emergency situations.

Emergency Preparedness

With some advance planning, you can increase the chances that your Sheltie and other pets will survive an emergency, whether you are there or not. Here are some tips:

- Post a sign listing your pets on or near your front and back doors. Stickers for that purpose are available from many vets, shelters, and other sources, or you can make one yourself. If your pets are crated or confined to specific parts of the house, include that information, as well as the location of their collars or harnesses.

- Arrange a safe drop-off site with a friend, relative, or veterinary clinic so that you or a rescuer know where to take your pets for temporary safe keeping. If you live in an area that is prone to natural disasters, make backup arrangements for veterinary care and boarding in case the disaster affects your regular vet.

- Make sure your Sheltie has a secure crate so that he can be safely controlled and transported, and make sure he has current identification.

- Keep a clearly labeled pet evacuation kit in a portable waterproof container and store it where it's easy to access. Include some or all of the following: important phone numbers (your office and cell phone, your vet, and others); copies of your dog's rabies certificate and other veterinary records; your Sheltie's medications, including heartworm preventative; proof of ownership in case someone else rescues your dog (a good color photo, and copies of your Sheltie's license registration, microchip and/or tattoo numbers, veterinary records, registration certificates, or purchase or adoption papers); feeding instructions and health care needs; a week's supply of dog food sealed in air-tight bags or containers, and one or two bottles of water (rotate food and water once a month with fresh supplies); enough cash or travelers' checks to pay for boarding your dogs for at least three days. Hopefully, you'll never need your evacuation kit, but if you ever do, you'll be glad you have it.

First Aid

Most people find it reassuring and occasionally useful to have first-aid supplies on hand. You can purchase a ready-made pet first-aid kit, but it's less costly to assemble one yourself. Here's what you need:

- a muzzle that fits your dog
- 3% hydrogen peroxide (write the purchase date on the label, and discard and replace the bottle once a year)
- a medicine syringe (without the needle) for administering liquids
- antidiarrheal medication (ask your veterinarian for recommendations)
- a small rectal thermometer and a sterile lubricant (*not* petroleum jelly)
- sterile saline eye solution to flush eyes
- a broad-spectrum antibiotic cream
- a small bottle of mild liquid dish detergent to remove contaminants from coat and skin
- disposable gloves in case you need to handle a contaminated dog

- scissors
- tweezers
- a veterinary first-aid manual (ask your veterinarian or local Red Cross for recommendations)
- directions and telephone numbers for your regular veterinarian and the closest emergency veterinary clinic
- the telephone number for the National Animal Poison Control Center (NAPCC): 1-888-4ANI-HELP or 1-900-680-0000

Store your supplies in a plastic box with a handle and secure closure. Label it clearly, and keep it where it's easy to find. Take it along if you travel with your dog, or keep a second kit in the car.

If you find yourself faced with a canine emergency, protect yourself and other people first (an injured, ill, or frightened dog may hurt you without meaning to, and some emergencies involve external hazards such as traffic), then focus on helping your dog. Act quickly, but don't panic.

This is only very basic information, so consider buying a good book on veterinary first aid to keep with your first-aid kit, or take a course on pet first aid from your local Red Cross or other source. Now let's look at some common canine emergencies.

Bites, Scratches, and Bleeding

Bites, scratches, and other wounds aren't unusual in active dogs, especially those who play with other animals. A minor wound should be cleaned gently with water and a clean cloth. If it bleeds, apply direct pressure with a clean towel, cloth, or gauze pad. Do *not* put hydrogen peroxide on an open wound—it can damage the tissue and promote bleeding. When the wound stops bleeding, apply a broad-spectrum antibiotic, then call your vet. Even minor wounds are susceptible to infection, and your dog may need additional antibiotics. If your Sheltie is bitten by a wild or stray animal, make sure his rabies vaccinations are current. (See also "Rabies.")

If a wound won't stop bleeding, or it is deep, long, or dirty, seek immediate veterinary attention. If possible, have someone drive you to the vet so that you can maintain pressure to control the bleeding. If you're alone, put your dog in a crate to keep him secure. Tape a gauze pad or clean towel to the wound if

Emergency first-aid procedures can increase your dog's chances of a full recovery—and may even save his life.

necessary, but do *not* apply a tourniquet unless you have had first-aid training—you could cause serious, permanent damage. Keep other animals away from the injured animal.

Even with proper care and antibiotics, infection is always possible when skin is broken, so check the wound every day for a week or so, and call your vet if you see any swelling, tenderness, or other signs of infection, or if your dog shows other signs of illness.

Broken Bones or Other Injuries

Fractures—broken bones—are not uncommon in active, playful dogs. A compound fracture in which the bone breaks through the skin is obvious, but not all fractures are apparent without x-rays.

Fractures need veterinary care as soon as possible to relieve pain and prevent further damage. If you think your Sheltie may have broken a bone, wrap him gently but securely in a blanket or towel, being careful not to disturb the injury. If possible, use a blanket or board to move him so that the bone remains stable. Keep your dog (and yourself!) as calm as possible, and get him to the vet.

Treatment will depend on the type and severity of the fracture, its location, and your dog's age and general health. Simple breaks often heal quickly with the help of a simple walking cast, but others may require surgery and supportive metal plates or pins.

Heatstroke

Heatstroke (hyperthermia) can occur if your dog's body temperature exceeds the safe range (99.5° to 102.8°F [37.5° to 39.3°C]) for even a few minutes. Heatstroke can kill your Sheltie or cause serious, permanent injury, and his heavy coat puts him at special risk in hot weather. The only way he can cool his body is by panting, a rather inefficient method in warm weather. If you are out with your dog and notice that he is panting heavily, let him rest and cool off in a shady spot periodically. You can help him cool down by wetting his belly and the pads of his feet with cool water. (Don't wet his entire body because as the water in his coat evaporates, it will create a steam bath around him.)

Symptoms of heatstroke include red or pale gums; bright red tongue; thick, sticky saliva; rapid panting; vomiting and/or diarrhea; dizziness; weakness; and shock. If you think your Sheltie is suffering from heatstroke, wrap him in a cool, wet towel or blanket and get him to a veterinarian as quickly as possible. In warm weather, *never* leave your Sheltie in a parked vehicle. Even with the windows partly opened, the temperature inside a stationary vehicle can reach lethal levels in a matter of minutes.

Poisoning

If you know or suspect that your Sheltie has been poisoned, contact your veterinarian or an emergency vet clinic immediately. Do not wait for symptoms to appear—by then, it may be too late. If possible, take the container or a sample of the substance with you, or write down the active ingredients, brand name, manufacturer's name and telephone number, and any antidote information provided on the package. Your vet may administer an antidote, fluids, or other treatments, depending on the poison, how much your dog ingested, and how long it's been since he was exposed. Your dog may also need supportive care and close monitoring for some time.

Sometimes dogs get into things without their owners' knowledge. Signs of poisoning may appear quickly or after some time, depending on the poison, the dose relative to the dog's size, and other factors. Common signs of poisoning include one or more of the following: vomiting, diarrhea, loss of appetite, swelling of the tongue and other mouth tissues, excessive salivation, staggering, or seizures. If your Sheltie displays any of these, call your vet. You can also contact the National Animal Poison Control Center (NAPCC) for emergency advice at 1-888-4ANI-HELP or 1-900-680-000 (a nominal fee is charged per call).

YOUR SENIOR SHELTIE

Aging can't be stopped, but it's effects can often be delayed with good care. Some medical problems cause premature aging, and your vet may be able to treat those, thus lengthening your Sheltie's life and improving its quality, at least for a while. High-quality food, regular reasonable exercise, and lots of love and affection will also help make your Sheltie's senior years good ones.

As your dog ages, give your vet detailed information about changes in his physical health and behavior. If something goes wrong, discuss your options. Before you opt for an expensive or invasive procedure, consider how long your dog's life may be prolonged and how much he will enjoy it. Longer is not always better. The financial and emotional cost of extensive veterinary care can be high, too, so be honest with yourself and with your vet about

Signs of Aging

- arthritis or joint stiffness
- circulatory problems
- decreased kidney function
- dental problems
- ear infections
- lower energy level
- reduced vision or hearing
- skin or fleshy tumors
- weight loss or weight gain

your ability to take on the financial, physical, and emotional costs of special or extraordinary care.

With proper nutrition, exercise, and regular vet visits, most Shelties remain healthy and active well into their second decades. Just remember that old dogs need your love and attention as much as young ones. As he ages, your Sheltie may stiffen up and lose his eyesight and hearing, but the same loving heart lives within.

SAYING GOODBYE

Farewells to even the oldest of dogs come much too soon. In the midst of loss and grief, though, it's good to know that, when the time comes, we can spare our dogs, whatever their age, from suffering and give them a dignified end.

When chronic illness, irreparable injury, or old age rob your Sheltie of his quality of life, it may be time to discuss euthanasia with your vet. It's never an easy decision, but it is a loving one. Your dog will nearly always tell you when it's time.

The euthanasia process is fast and virtually painless. If you have not been through this before, ask your vet to tell you as much as you want to know to be comfortable with your decision. Give each family member a chance to say farewell. Very young children should probably not be present for the euthanasia itself, but they should be able to ask questions and express their feelings.

Whether you want to be present is, of course, your decision, but if you can, your dog will be more relaxed if he knows you're there. If you or other family members want time alone with your dog after the procedure, tell your vet, and let her know how you want your dog's remains to be handled.

Few things in life bring more pain than the loss of a beloved dog. Unfortunately, some people don't understand, and some may say stupid things. Avoid them. Spend time with your pets and with people who understand. Be kind to yourself, and give yourself time to grieve. If you feel you need support to get through the grieving process, join a pet-loss support group in your community or on the Internet (ask your vet, or call your local animal shelter for information).

ASSOCIATIONS AND ORGANIZATIONS

American Herding Breed Association

1548 Victoria Way
Pacifica, CA 94044
Telephone: (415) 355-9563
www.ahba-herding.org

American Shetland Sheepdog Association

3921 Donner Trail
Placerville, CA 95667-9218
Telephone: (530) 626-6160
www.assa.org

BREED CLUBS

American Kennel Club (AKC)

5580 Centerview Drive
Raleigh, NC 27606
Telephone: (919) 233-9767
Fax: (919) 233-3627
E-mail: info@akc.org
www.akc.org

Canadian Kennel Club (CKC)

89 Skyway Avenue,
Suite 100
Etobicoke, Ontario
M9W 6R4
Canada
Telephone: (416) 675-5511
Fax: (416) 675-6506
E-mail: information@ckc.ca
www.ckc.ca

Federation Cynologique Internationale (FCI)

Secretariat General de la FCI
Place Albert 1er, 13
B – 6530 Thuin
Belgique
www.fci.be

The Kennel Club

1 Clarges Street
London
W1J 8AB
England
Telephone: 0870 606 6750
Fax: 0207 518 1058
www.the-kennel-club.org.uk

United Kennel Club (UKC)

100 E. Kilgore Road
Kalamazoo, MI 49002-5584
Telephone: (269) 343-9020
Fax: (269) 343-7037
E-mail: pbickell@ukcdogs.com
www.ukcdogs.com

PET SITTERS

National Association of Professional Pet Sitters

15000 Commerce Parkway,
Suite C
Mt. Laurel, NJ 08054
Telephone: (856) 439-0324
Fax: (856) 439-0525
E-mail: napps@ahint.com
www.petsitters.org

Pet Sitters International

201 East King Street
King, NC 27021-9161
Telephone: (336) 983-9222
Fax: (336) 983-5266
E-mail: info@petsit.com
www.petsit.com

RESCUE ORGANIZATIONS AND ANIMAL WELFARE GROUPS

American Humane Association (AHA)

63 Inverness Drive East
Englewood, CO 80112
Telephone: (303) 792-9900
Fax: 792-5333
www.americanhumane.org

American Society for the Prevention of Cruelty to Animals (ASPCA)

424 E. 92nd Street
New York, NY 10128-6804
Telephone: (212) 876-7700
www.aspca.org

Royal Society for the Prevention of Cruelty to Animals (RSPCA)

Telephone: 0870 3335 999
Fax: 0870 7530 284
www.rspca.org.uk

Canine Freestyle Federation, Inc.
E-mail: secretary@canine-freestyle.org
www.canine-freestyle.org

International Agility Link (IAL)
Global Administrator: Steve Drinkwater
E-mail: yunde@powerup.au
www.agilityclick.com/~ial

North American Dog Agility Council
11522 South Hwy 3
Cataldo, ID 83810
www.nadac.com

North American Flyball Association
1400 West Devon Avenue #512
Chicago, IL 60660
800-318-6312
www.flyball.org

United States Dog Agility Association
P.O. Box 850955
Richardson, TX 75085-0955
Telephone: (972) 487-2200
www.usdaa.com

World Canine Freestyle Organization
P.O. Box 350122
Brooklyn, NY 11235-2525
Telephone: (718) 332-8336
www.worldcaninefreestyle.org

THERAPY

Delta Society
875 124th Ave NE, Suite 101
Bellevue, WA 98005
Telephone: (425) 226-7357
Fax: (425) 235-1076
E-mail: info@deltasociety.org
www.deltasociety.org

Therapy Dogs Incorporated
P.O. Box 5868
Cheyenne, WY 82003
Telephone: (877) 843-7364
E-mail: therdog@sisna.com
www.therapydogs.com

Therapy Dogs International (TDI)
88 Bartley Road
Flanders, NJ 07836
Telephone: (973) 252-9800
Fax: (973) 252-7171
E-mail: tdi@gti.net
www.tdi-dog.org

TRAINING

Animal Behavior Society
www.animalbehavior.org

Association of Pet Dog Trainers (APDT)
150 Executive Center Drive
Box 35
Greenville, SC 29615
Telephone: (800) PET-DOGS
Fax: (864) 331-0767
E-mail: information@apdt.com
www.apdt.com

National Association of Dog Obedience Instructors (NADOI)
PMB 369
729 Grapevine Hwy.
Hurst, TX 76054-2085
www.nadoi.org

VETERINARY AND HEALTH RESOURCES

Academy of Veterinary Homeopathy (AVH)
P.O. Box 9280
Wilmington, DE 19809
Telephone: (866) 652-1590
Fax: (866) 652-1590
E-mail: office@TheAVH.org
www.theavh.org

American Academy of Veterinary Acupuncture (AAVA)
100 Roscommon Drive, Suite 320
Middletown, CT 06457
Telephone: (860) 635-6300
Fax: (860) 635-6400
E-mail: office@aava.org
www.aava.org

American Animal Hospital Association (AAHA)
P.O. Box 150899
Denver, CO 80215-0899
Telephone: (303) 986-2800
Fax: (303) 986-1700
E-mail: info@aahanet.org
www.aahanet.org/index.cfm

American College of Veterinary Internal Medicine (ACVIM)
1997 Wadsworth Blvd., Suite A
Lakewood, CO 80214-5293
Telephone: (800) 245-9081
Fax: (303) 231-0880
E-mail: ACVIM@ACVIM.org
www.acvim.org

American College of Veterinary Ophthalmologists (ACVO)
P.O. Box 1311
Meridian, ID 83860
Telephone: (208) 466-7624
Fax: (208) 466-7693
E-mail: office@acvo.com
www.acvo.com

American Holistic Veterinary Medical Association (AHVMA)
2218 Old Emmorton Road
Bel Air, MD 21015
Telephone: (410) 569-0795
Fax: (410) 569-2346
E-mail: office@ahvma.org
www.ahvma.org

American Veterinary Medical Association (AVMA)
1931 North Meacham Road, Suite 100
Schaumburg, IL 60173
Telephone: (847) 925-8070
Fax: (847) 925-1329
E-mail: avmainfo@avma.org
www.avma.org

ASPCA Animal Poison Control Center
1717 South Philo Road, Suite 36
Urbana, IL 61802
Telephone: (888) 426-4435
www.aspca.org

British Veterinary Association (BVA)
7 Mansfield Street
London
W1G 9NQ
England
Telephone: 020 7636 6541
Fax: 020 7436 2970
E-mail: bvahq@bva.co.uk
www.bva.co.uk

Canine Eye Registration Foundation (CERF)
VMDB/CERF
1248 Lynn Hall
625 Harrison St.
Purdue University
West Lafayette, IN 47907-2026
Telephone: (765) 494-8179
E-mail: CERF@vmbd.org
www.vmdb.org

Orthopedic Foundation for Animals (OFA)
2300 NE Nifong Blvd.
Columbus, MI 65201-3856
Telephone: (573) 442-0418
Fax: (573) 875-5073
E-mail: ofa@offa.org
www.offa.org

PUBLICATIONS

Books

Boneham, Sheila Webster. *Training Your Dog for Life.* Neptune City, T.F.H. Publications, 2008.

Goldstein, Robert S., V.M.D., and Susan J. *The Goldsteins' Wellness & Longevity Program.* Neptune City: T.F.H. Publications, 2005.

Morgan, Diane. *Good Dogkeeping.* Neptune City: T.F.H. Publications, 2005.

MAGAZINES

AKC *Family Dog*
American Kennel Club
260 Madison Avenue
New York, NY 10016
Telephone: (800) 490-5675
E-mail: familydog@akc.org
www.akc.org/pubs/
familydog

AKC *Gazette*
American Kennel Club
260 Madison Avenue
New York, NY 10016
Telephone: (800) 533-7323
E-mail: gazette@akc.org
www.akc.org/pubs/gazette

Dog & Kennel
Pet Publishing, Inc.
7-L Dundas Circle
Greensboro, NC 27407
Telephone: (336) 292-4272
Fax: (336) 292-4272
E-mail: info@petpublishing.
com
www.dogandkennel.com

Dog Fancy
Subscription Department
P.O. Box 53264
Boulder, CO 80322-3264
Telephone: (800) 365-4421
E-mail: barkback@dogfancy.
com
www.dogfancy.com

Dogs Monthly
Ascot House
High Street, Ascot,
Berkshire SL5 7JG
United Kingdom
Telephone: 0870 730 8433
Fax: 0870 730 8431
E-mail: admin@rtc-
associates.freeserve.co.uk
www.corsini.co.uk/
dogsmonthly

Note: **Boldfaced** numbers indicate illustrations.

A

AAA (animal-assisted activities), 139
AAHA (American Animal Hospital Association), 200
AAT (animal-assisted therapy), 139
AAVA (American Academy of Veterinary Acupuncture), 199
abnormal growths, 178
Academy of Veterinary Homopathy (AVH), 199
accidents during housetraining, 102–103
acepromazine, 161
activities. See advanced training and activities
acupuncture, 189
ACVIM (American College of Veterinary Internal Medicine), 200
ACVO (American College of Veterinary Ophthalmologists), 200
ADD (Advanced Disc Dog) title, 144
adolescent dogs, feeding, 65, 67
adoption, 40–43
adult dogs
  feeding, 65, 67
  housetraining, 101–104
  retraining, 129
  training, 96
adult vs. puppy Shelties, 31–33, **32**
Advanced Disc Dog (ADD) title, 144
advanced training and activities, 131–151
  agility, 140, 149
  backpacking, 134–136
  bicycling with you Sheltie, 133
  canine musical freestyle, 144
  championship competition, 144–151, **147**
  conformation shows, 144–151, **147**
  dancing with dogs, 144
  flyball, 140
  flying disc competition, 143–144
  herding events, 143, 149
  hiking, 134–136
  jogging, 131–136
  noncompetitive, 131–136, **132**
  obedience competition, 141–142, 149
  performance dogs, 148–151
  performance sports, 140–151, **141**
  rally competition, 141–142, 149

running, 131–136
safety rules for, 133
stockdog events, 143
titles for competitive events, 149
tracking competition, 142–143, 149
volunteer activities, 138–139
walking, 131–136
age appropriate time for homecoming, 46–47
aggression, 115–116
agility competition, 140, 149
aging, signs of, 196
AHBA (American Herding Breed Association), 142, 143
AHVMA (American Holistic Veterinary Medical Association), 155, 191, 200
air travel, 51
AKC (American Kennel Club). See American Kennel Club (AKC)
AKC Campion (CH) title, 146
AKC Canine Good Citizen (CGC) program, 136–138, **137**
AKC Family Dog (magazine), 201
AKC Gazette (magazine), 201
allergies, 161, 174–176, **175**
alternative practitioners, 191
alternative therapies, 189–191
America Humane Association (AMA), 198
American Academy of Veterinary Acupuncture (AAVA), 199
American Animal Hospital Association (AAHA), 200
American College of Veterinary Internal Medicine (ACVIM), 200
American College of Veterinary Ophthalmologists (ACVO), 200
American Herding Breed Association (AHBA), 142, 143, 198
American Holistic Veterinary Medical Association (AHVMA), 155, 191, 200
American Kennel Club (AKC)
  conformation program, 145, 146
  contact information, 10, 198
  herding test and trials, 143
  history of, 8
  spaying and neutering and, 173
  standards, 14
  titles, types of, 149
American Shelties, 9
American Shetland Sheepdog Association (ASSA), 9, 35, 173, 198
American Society for the Prevention of Cruelty to Animals (ASPCA), 198
American Veterinary Medical

Association (AVMA), 155, 200
anal glands, 83
anal sac care, 89
anaplasmosis, 172
Animal Behavior Society, 199
animal welfare groups, 198
animal-assisted activities (AAA), 139
animal-assisted therapy (AAT), 139
annual checkups, 155–156
anxiety, 116–119
APDT (Association of Pet Dog Trainers), 116, 142, 199
ASCA (Australian Shepherd Club of America), 142, 143
ASPCA (American Society for the Prevention of Cruelty to Animals), 198
ASPCA Animal Poison Control Center, 200
ASSA (American Shetland Sheepdog Association), 9, 173, 198
Association of Pet Dog Trainers (APDT), 116, 142, 199
Australian Shepherd Club of America (ASCA), 142, 143
autoimmune diseases, 176–177
autoimmune lymphocytic thyroiditis, 176–177
AVH (Academy of Veterinary Homopathy), 199
AVID Microchips, 49
AVMA (American Veterinary Medical Association), 155, 200

B

babesiosis, 172
backpacking activities, 134–136
balance, definition of, 19
bark collars, 121–122
barking, 26, 33, 119–122, **121**
Basic Disc Dog (BDD) title, 143–144
bath supplies, 80, **81**
bathing, 80–83, **81**, **82**
BDD (Basic Disc Dog) title, 143–144
BEAR (Brainstem Auditory Evoked Response) test, 181, 182
begging, 70
behavior
  problems, 114–129, **114**
  training and, 93–129
  traits, 24–26, **25**, 33
benign tumor, 178
Best in Show (BIS) title, 146
Best of Breed (BOB) title, 145–146
Best of Opposite Sex (BOS) title, 145
Best of Winners (BOW) title, 145
bi-black, coat color, 20
bi-blue, coat color, 21

bicycling with you Sheltie, 133
BIS (Best in Show) title, 146
bites, 193–194
biting, 115–116, 126–127
black, coat color, 20
bleeding, 193–194
Blind Dogs (association), 182
blue merle, coat color, 20–21
boarding
    feeding and, 64–65
    options, 52–53, **52**
BOB (Best of Breed) title, 145–146
body, characteristics of, 17–18
Boneham, Sheila Webster, 200
Border Collie, 6, 8
bordetella, 158
BOS (Best of Opposite Sex) title,
    145
BOW (Best of Winners) title, 145
bowls, 48
Brainstem Auditory Evoked
    Response (BEAR) test, 181, 182
breed champion title, 146
breed clubs, 198
breed standards, 13–14
breeders, 36–40, **38**
    health guarantees, 37–38
    health screenings, 39
    quality and cost, 38, 40
    visiting, 36
breeding practices, 16, 26, 35–36
British Veterinary Association
    (BVA), 200
broken bones, 194–195
brushes, 75–76
brushing
    coat, 77–79, **79**
    teeth, 84–85
burrs, dealing with, 78–79
Butcher Boy (Sheltie), 8
butorphanol, 161
BVA (British Veterinary
    Association), 200

C
Canadian Kennel Club (CKC), 198
cancers, canine, 177–178
Canine Cancer Awareness, Inc.,
    155
Canine Epilepsy Network, 155
Canine Eye Registry Foundation
    (CERF), 182, 200
Canine Freestyle Federation, Inc.,
    199
Canine Good Citizen (CGC)
    program, 136–138, **137**
canine musical freestyle, 144
canned dog food, 60
car travel, 50–51, **51**
carbohydrates, 56
carcinoma, 178
cataracts, 86, 182–183
cats and Shelties, 29, **29**
CEA (collie eye anomaly), 39,

183–184
ceramic bowls, 48
CERF (Canine Eye Registry
    Foundation), 182, 200
CGC (Canine Good Citizen)
    program, 136–138, **137**
Ch. Ashbank Fairy (Sheltie), 11
Ch. Blaeberry of Clerwood
    (Sheltie), 11
Ch. Lerwick Rex (Sheltie), 11
Ch. Peabody Pan (Sheltie), 11
Ch. Walesby Select (Sheltie), 9
Ch. Wee Laird O'Downfield
    (Sheltie), 11
chain leashes, 49
championship competition,
    144–151, **147**
characteristics of the Sheltie, 13–29
chasing, 33
chemical hazards, 47–48, **175**
Chestnut Blossom (Sheltie), 11
Chestnut Bud (Sheltie), 11
Chestnut Garland (Sheltie), 11
Chestnut Lucky Boy (Sheltie), 11
Chestnut Rainbow (Sheltie), 11
chew toys, 84, 101, 123
chewing, 122–124, **123**
cheyletiella, 171
children and Shelties, 27–28
    basic rules for, 28
    during play time, 99
    during shelter visits, 43
    during training, 107
    while feeding, 73
chiropractic treatment, 189–190,
    190
CKC (Canadian Kennel Club), 198
coat
    care of, 77–83
    characteristics of, 5, **18**, 19–24
coccidia, 165
collars, 49, 121–122, 186, 187
collie eye anomaly (CEA), 39,
    183–184
Collie's, 6, 7, 8
color-headed whites, coat color, 23
colors of Shelties, 19–21, **22**
Combined Skills Freestyle (CSF)
    title, 144
combs, 76
Come command, 107–109, **109**
commands, 107–114
commercial dog foods, 58–61
Companion Animal Recovery, 49
competition dogs, 34–35
competitive sports, 26
conditioners, 76–77
conditioning program, 132
conformation shows, 144–151, **147**
conjunctivitis, 185
Cornell University College of
    Veterinary Medicine Information
    Resources, 155
coronavirus, 157–158

cost, 40
crate training, 99–101
crates
    requirements for, 99–100, **100**
    selection criteria, 48, 49
    while traveling, 50–51
cryptic merle, coat color, 23
CSF (Combined Skills Freestyle)
    title, 144

D
dancing with dogs, 144
DDX (Disc Dog Expert), 144
Deaf Dog Education Action Fund
    (DDEAF), 182
debarking procedure, 120
Delta Society, 139, 199
demodex mites, 170
dental
    care, 83–85
    checkups, 84
    exam, 83
dental care tools, 75–77, **76**
dew claws, 18, 88
dewormers, 168
digging, **114**, 115
Disc Dog Expert (DDX), 144
discoid lupus erythematosus
    (DLE), 176
distemper, 158
Dog & Kennel (magazine), 201
Dog Fancy (magazine), 201
doggy breath, 83
doggy day care, 52–53, **52**
Dogs Monthly (magazine), 201
double merle, coat color, 23, 24
Down command, 111–112
Downfield Grethe (Sheltie), 11
doxorubicin, 161
Dremel tool, 88, 89
drugs, sensitivity (allergies) to,
    161
dry dog food, 59, **59**
dryers, 77
drying you Sheltie, 83
Dutch, pattern of markings, 23

E
ear problems
    deafness, 23, 24, 180–181
    infections, 83, 178
    injuries, 178–180
ears
    care of, 85–86, **85**
    characteristics of, 17
    cleaners for, 77
    health issues, 23, 24
East Coast fever, 172
ehrlichia, 172
Elizabethan collar, 186, 187
emergency care, 191–196, **194**
emergency preparedness, 192
end of life issues, 197

Eng. Ch. Redbraes Magda (Sheltie), 11
environment, physical, 26–27
etiquette while traveling, 51
euthanasia, 197
exercise, 27, 33, 72–73, **72**, 115, 133
external parasites, **164**, 168–173
eye problems
    cataracts, 182–183
    collie eye anomaly, 183–184
    infections, 184–185
    injuries, 185–186
    merle ocular dysgenesis, 23, 24, 184, **184**
eyes
    care of, **85**, 86–87
    characteristics of, 17, 21
    exam for, 39

F

Farburn Dinnah (Dinah) (Sheltie), 10
fats, 56
fear, 116–119
fecal sample, collecting, 165
Federation Cynologique Internationale (FCI), 198
feeding, 55–73, **72**
    commercial dog foods, 58–60
    frequency for, by age, 65
    noncommercial dog foods, 61–64
    nutrients, 55–58
    schedules, 64–69, **64**
    weight control and, 69–73
female vs. male Shelties, 33–34
first aid, 192–193, **194**
fitness, 131–136
flat brushes, 75
flatulence, 83
flea-prevention products, 77
fleas, 82, 169, **171**
flyball, 140
flying disc competition, 143–144
food. *See also* feeding
    allergies, 175–176
    appropriateness of, 48
    labels, 61
foot care, 87–89
forequarters, characteristics of, 18–19
free feeding schedule, 64–65
freestyle, canine musical, 144

G

giardia, 166
gingivitis, 84
Goldstein, Robert S., 200
Goldstein, Susan J., 200
The Goldsteins' Wellness & Longevity Program (Goldstein), 200
Good Dogkeeping (Morgan), 200

Great Britain, history of Shelties in, 7–8
grooming, 75–91
    benefits of, 75
    coat care, 77–83
    for competition, 148
    dental care, 83–85
    ear care, 85–86
    eye care, 86–87
    foot care, 87–89
    as health check, 78
    nail care, 87–89
    professional, 89–91, **90**
    supplies for, 49
growling, 115–116
guarding, 128–129, **128**
gum disease, 83–84

H

Hailes Princess (Sheltie), 10
hair dryers, 77
handlers, professional, 147–148
head, 16–17
health, 153–196
    alternative therapies, 189–191
    emergency care, 191–196, **194**
    first aid, 192–193, **194**
    grooming as check for, 78
    guarantees, 37–38
    resources for, 199–200
    screenings, 39
    signs of healthy puppies, 45
health issues, 153–197, **179**
    allergies, 161, 174–176, **175**
    autoimmune diseases, 176–177
    bacterial diseases, **159**
    broken bones, 194–195
    cancers, 177–178
    cataracts, 182–183
    collie eye anomaly, 39, 183–184
    ear problems, 85–86, 178–181
    hearing problems, 23, 24
    heatstroke, 195
    hot spots, 186–188, **187**
    infectious diseases, 156–162
    injuries, 194–195
    merle ocular dysgenesis, 23, 184
    online resources for, 155
    parasites, 162–173, **164**
    periodontal disease, 81–82, 84
    poisoning, 195–196
    prescription diets for, 60–61
    thyroid disease, 39, 176–177, 188–189
    types of, 36
    vaccinations, 156–162, **157**
    white Shelties and, 22–23
hearing problems, 23, 24, 180–181, 182
hearing tests, 180–181
heartworm disease, 162–163
heatstroke, 195
hematoma, 179

hepatitis, infectious canine, 158
herbal therapy, 190
herding events, 143, 149
herding Tested (HT) title, 143
heterozygous merles, 23, 24
hiking activities, 134–136
hindquarters, characteristics of, 18–19
hip dysplasia, testing for, 39
history of Shelties, 5–11, **7**
home cooked diet foods, 62–63, **62**
HomeAgain MicroChips, 49
homecoming, 46–48
    age appropriate time for, 46–47
    preparing home and yard for, 47–48, **47**
homeopathy, 190–191
hookworms, 166
hot spots, 186–188, **187**
household rules, establishing, 97
houseplants, 47
housetraining, 101–104, **103**
    feeding and, 65–66
    tips for, 104
Humphries, E. P., 10
hyperthyroidism, 188–189
hypothyroidism, 188–189

I

IAL (International Agility Link), 199
IDDHA (International Disc Dog Handlers' Association), 143
identification tags, 49
Individual Limited Privileges (ILP) status, 142
infectious canine hepatitis, 158
infectious diseases, 156–162
influential dogs and people, 9–11, **9**
injuries, 194–195
International Agility Link (IAL), 199
International Disc Dog Handlers' Association (IDDHA), 143
intestinal gas, 83
intestinal parasites, 163–168, **164**, **167**
Inverness Yarrow (Sheltie), 9
Irish, pattern of markings, 23
ivermectin, 161

J

Jarl, Lerwick, 11
jogging activities, 131–136
jumping up, 124–126, **126**

K

Kennel Club (KC), 7, 9, 10, 198
kennel cough, 158
kibble, 59
Kilravock Laddie (Sheltie), 9
Knott's test, 162
Ko-Ko (Sheltie), 11

L

leash training, 104–105, **105**
leashes, 49, 135
lens-induced uveitis (LIU), 183
leptospirosis, 159
loperamide, 161
Lord Scott (Sheltie), 8
lump, 178
Lyme disease, 159–160, 172

M

male vs. female Shelties, 33–34
malignant tumor, 178
malnutrition, 58
mange, 170–171
marking territories, 34
markings on Shelties, 21–22
Master Disc Dog (MDD) title, 144
mating behaviors, 34
mats
    dealing with, 78–79
    splitters for, 76
MCSI (Musical Canine Sports
    International), 144
MDD (Master Disc Dog) title, 144
MDR1 (multi-drug resistance)
    mutation, 161
medicines, sensitivity (allergies)
    to, 161
merle, coat color, 20–21, 23
merle ocular dysgenesis, 23, 184
metal combs, 76
metastasize, 178
microchips, 49
milbemycin, 161
minerals, 57
mites, 170–171, **171**
Morgan, Diane, 200
mouthing, 126–127
moxidectin, 161
multi-drug resistance (MDR1)
    mutation, 161
Musical Canine Sports
    International (MCSI), 144
musical freestyle, canine, 144

N

NADAC (North American Dog
    Agility Council), 142, 199
NADOI (National Association of
    Dog Obedience Instructors), 199
nail care, 87–89
nail clippers, 76, **87**
naming convention for dogs, 17
Natalie of Clerwood (Sheltie), 11
National Animal Poison Control
    Center (NAPCC), 193, 196
National Association of Dog
    Obedience Instructors (NADOI),
    199
National Association of
    Professional Pet Sitters, 198
National Dog Registry, 49
neck, characteristics of, 17–18

neoplasm, 178
neutering, 34, 173–174, 177
noncommercial dog foods, 61–64
noncompetitive activities, 131–
    136, **132**
North American Dog Agility
    Council (NADAC), 142, 199
North American Flyball
    Association, 199
nuclear sclerosis, 86
Nut of Houghton Hill (Sheltie), 11
nutrition, **68**. *See also* feeding; food
    requirements for, 55–58, **56**
    therapy and, 191
Nylabone, 69, **71**, **72**, 83, 84, 95,
    101, 123, 124, 127, 143
nylon collars, 49

O

obedience
    classes, 106–107
    competition, 141–142
    titles for, 149
obesity, 67–68
odors, controlling, 83
ophthalmic ointment, 81–82
Orthopedic Foundation for
    Animals (OFA), 200

P

paper training, 103–104
paperwork, 44–45
parainfluenza, 160
parasites, 162–173, **164**
parvovirus (parvo), 160
Pedro (Sheltie), 10
performance dogs, 148–151
performance sports, 140–151, **141**
periodontal disease, 84
pet qualities in Shelties, 34, **35**
pet sitters, **52**, 53, 198
Pet Sitters International, 198
pet-proofing home and yard,
    47–48, **47**
pets and Shelties, 29, **29**
PETtrac, 49
pin brushes, 75
plastic bowls, 48
poisoning, 195–196
positive training, 95–96
potty training, 46
pounds, **41**, 42–43
PRA (Progressive Retinal
    Atrophy), 39
praise words, 97
preparing for you sheltie, 31–53
prescription diets, 60–61
Printfield Bess (Sheltie), 11
private adoptions, 43
professional
    groomers, 89–91, **90**
    handlers, 147–148
    trainers, 105–107
Progressive Retinal Atrophy

(PRA), 39
proteins, 57
punishment, 96
puppies
    vs. adult Sheltie, **29**, 31–33
    feeding, 65, 66
    healthy signs for, 45
puppy kindergarten, 106

Q

quality and cost, 38, 40

R

rabies, 157, 161–162
rally competition, 141–142, 149
raw diets, 63–64
red sable, coat color, 20
Redbraes Rollo (Sheltie), 11
relapsing fever, 172
release words, 97
rescue organizations, 198
rescue programs, 40–42, **41**
resource guarding, 128–129, **128**
restraint collar, 186, 187
retractable leashes, 135
retraining, 129
rewards, 95–96
ringworm, 171–172
Rip of Mountfort (Sheltie), 10
Rocky Mountain spotted fever,
    172
Rose, Badenock, 7
Rough Collies, 6, 7
roundworms, 166–167
Royal Society for the Prevention
    of Cruelty to Animals (RSPCA),
    198
running activities, 131–136
rusting, coat color, 20

S

sable, coat color, 20
sable merle, coat color, 21
safety rules, 28, 133
sarcoma, 178
sarcoptic mites, 170–171
Saunders, J. G., 10
scabies, 170–171
scheduled feeding, **64**, 65–66
scissors, 76
scratches, 193–194
sedatives, 91
selamectin, 161
selection criteria, **44**, 45–46
selective breeding, 26
self blue, coat color, 21
semi-moist dog food, 59–60
senior dogs
    care of, 196–197
    dietary needs, 63
    eye problems, 86
    feeding and, 65, 67–69
separation anxiety, 117–118, **118**
service dogs, 138–139

SES (Sheltie Eye Syndrome), 39
shaded sable, coat color, 20
shampoos, 76–77, **82**, 83
shears, thinning, 76
shedding, 20, 33
shelters, **41**, 42–43
Sheltie Eye Syndrome (SES), 39
Sherman, John G. Jr., 8
show dogs, 34–35
    grooming for, 91
    locating, 148–151
Silverlining (Sheltie), 11
Sit command, 109–111, **110**
size of Shelties, 9, 14–16, **15**
Skyhoundz, 144
socialization, 26, 32, 98, **98**
spaying, 34, 173–174, 177
special formula commercial dog
    food, 60–61
sports associations, 199
stainless steel bowls, 48
Stay command, 112–114
stockdog events, 143
stomach gas, 83
styptic powder, 88
supplements, nutritional, 57
supplies, grooming, 49, 75–77

T

table scraps, 62
tangles, dealing with, 78–79
tapeworms, 167–168
tartar build-up, 84
Tattoo-A-Pet, 49
tattooing, 49
TDI (Therapy Dogs International),
    199
teething, 123, 124
temperament, 24–26, **25**, 33
therapy associations, 199
therapy dogs, 138–139
Therapy Dogs Incorporated, 139,
    199
Therapy Dogs International (TDI),
    139, 199
thinning shears, 76

thyroid disease, 39, 176–177,
    188–189
ticks, **171**, 172–173
Tina Teena of Mountfort (Sheltie),
    10–11
titles for competitive events, 149
Toonies, 6
tooth decay, 83–84
toothbrushes, 76
toothpaste, 76, 84
topline, characteristics of, 17–18
towels, 77
toys, 49–50
tracking competition, 142–143, 149
training, 75–91, 93–129, **94**
    associations, 199
    for bath, 81
    children and, 107
    classes for, 105–107
    commands for, 107–109
    crate, 99–101
    household rules, establishing,
    97
    housetraining, 101–104
    leash, 104–105, **105**
    for nail care, 88
    requirements for success, 94–95
    retraining, 129
    time to begin, 96–97
Training Your Dog for Life
    (Boneham), 200
traits, 24–26, 33
traveling with you Sheltie, 50–51,
    51, 64–65
treats, 48, 69, 71–72, **71**
tri-color, coat color, 20
tri-factored sable, coat color, 20
trimming
    coat, 79–80
    nails, 87–89, **87**
tumors, 177, 178

U

United Kennel Club (UKC), 10,
    142, 198

United States Dog Agility
    Association (USDAA), 142, 199
United States, history of Shelties
    in, 8–9

V

vaccinations, 156–162, **157**
versatility titles, 149
veterinarian, 153–156
    checkups, 42, **154**
    choosing, 153–155
    routine care, 155–156
veterinary ophthalmologist, 86,
    186
veterinary resources, 199–200
vinblastine, 161
vincristine, 161
vision problems, 23, 24, 86, 182
vitamins, 57
volunteer activities, 138–139
von Willebrand's Disease (vWD),
    testing for, 39

W

walking activities, 131–136
Wallace to Teena (Sheltie), 10
War Baby of Mountfort (Sheltie),
    10, 11
warning signals, 116
water requirements, 57–58, 68
WB (Winners' Bitch) title, 145
WCFO (World Canine Freestyle
    Organization), 144, 199
WD (Winners' Dog) title, 145
weight control, 69–73
Westminster, conformation show,
    145–146
wet dog food, 60
whipworms, 168
white, coat color, 22–24
Winners' Bitch (WB) title, 145
Winners' Dog (WD) title, 145
World Canine Freestyle
    Organization (WCFO), 144, 199
worms, 166–168

ABOUT THE AUTHOR

Sheila Webster Boneham, Ph.D., loves animals and writing about animals. Three of her books have won the prestigious Maxwell Award from the Dog Writers Association of America, including *The Simple Guide to Labrador Retrievers,* named Best Single Breed Book of 2002. Her cat books have also all won major awards from the Cat Writers' Association. Sheila seeks to educate people about pets through her writing and other activities. She and her canine companions are active in competition and in dog-assisted activities and therapy. A former university writing teacher, Sheila also conducts writing workshops. You can visit Sheila and her dogs on the web at www.sheilaboneham.com and on Facebook.

PHOTO CREDITS

Aaron Amat (Shutterstock): 58
Utekhina Anna (Shutterstock): 121
Matt Antonino (Shutterstock): 52
Andraz Cerar (Shutterstock): 103
Darlene Cutshall (Shutterstock): 168, 171
Bob Denelzen (Shutterstock): 25
Zhu Difeng (Shutterstock): 56
Andrew Fang (Shutterstock): 1
Andreas Gradin (Shutterstock): 125
Jostein Hauge (Shutterstock): 27, 179
James R. Hearn (Shutterstock): 115
Eric Isselée (Shutterstock): 88, 102, 106, 170, 177, 188
Ian Kahn: 12, 47, 71, 105, 109, 111, 129, 152, 163
Erik Lam (Shutterstock): 26, 108
Michael Ledray (Shutterstock); 128
George Lee (Shutterstock):
Sean MacD (Shutterstock): 104
V. J. Matthew (Shutterstock): 32, 74, 187
Patsy Michaud (Shutterstock): 135
Kati Molin (Shutterstock): 85, 118
Linda Muir (Shutterstock): 164
Ken Rieves: 207
Shutterstock: 36, 40, 42, 43, 60, 101, 139, 140, 162, 166, 175
teekaygee (Shutterstock): 190
TFH Archives: 4, 7, 9, 10, 11, 15, 22, 29, 30, 35, 38, 41, 44, 51, 54, 59, 64, 68, 72, 76, 79, 81, 82, 84, 87, 90, 92, 94, 98, 100, 110, 11, 119, 123, 126, 132, 134, 137, 141, 145, 147, 148, 149, 150, 154, 157, 159, 160, 167, 184, 194
HTuller (Shutterstock): 48
Graca Victoria (Shutterstock): 62, 181
Lynn Watson (Shutterstock): 173
Sidebars: Eric Isselée (Shutterstock); Kati Molin (Shutterstock); TFH Archives; Graca Victoria (Shutterstock); Lynn Watson (Shutterstock)

Front cover: TFH Archives
Back cover: Ian Kahn, TFH Archives

NATURAL with added VITAMINS
Nutri Dent® MD
Promotes Optimal Dental Health!

Visit nylabone.com
Join Club NYLA
for coupons &
product
information

360° Design
Cleaning Action!™
Dog's L♥ve'em!™
AVAILABLE IN MULTIPLE SIZES AND FLAVORS.

Nylabone®
Trusted For Over 40 Years

MADE IN THE USA

Our Mission with Nutri Dent® is to promote optimal dental health for dogs through a trusted, natural, delicious chew that provides effective cleaning action...GUARANTEED to make your dog go wild with anticipation and happiness!!!

Nylabone Products • P.O. Box 427, Neptune, NJ 07754-0427 • 1-800-631-2188 • Fax: 732-988-5466
www.nylabone.com • info@nylabone.com • For more information contact your sales representative or contact us at sales@tfh.com